Fred DeRuvo

http://www.studygrowknow.com

Behind Enemy Lines

Copyright © 2012 by Study-Grow-Know

All rights reserved. Written permission must be secured from the publisher to use or reproduce any part of this book, except brief quotations in critical reviews or articles.

Published in Scotts Valley, California, by Study-Grow-Know
www.studygrowknow.com • www.adroitpublications.com

Scripture quotations unless otherwise noted, are from The Holy Bible, New American Standard. Copyright © 1960, 1962, 1963, 1968, 1971, 1972, 1973, 1975, 1977, 1995 by The Lockman Foundation.

Images used in this publication (unless otherwise noted) are from clipartconnection.com and used with permission, ©2007 JUPITERIMAGES, and its licensors. All rights reserved.

Any Woodcuts used herein are in the Public Domain and free of copyright.

All Figure illustrations used in this book were created by the author and protected under copyright laws, © 2012, unless otherwise noted.

Cover Design and Interior Layout: Fred DeRuvo

Cover Photo: © Dusan Kostic - Fotolia.com

Editor: Hannah Brady

Library of Congress Cataloging-in-Publication Data

DeRuvo, Fred, 1957 –

ISBN 0988183307
EAN-13 978-0-9881833-0-8

1. Religion / Biblical Studies / General

CONTENTS

Foreword:	....	5
Chapter 1:	The Prince of Persia	14
Chapter 2:	Stargates in the Sky	22
Chapter 3:	Too Much Water Under the Bridge	33
Chapter 4:	The Overarching Problem	42
Chapter 5:	Ministries: Big Business	54
Chapter 6:	Looking Beyond the Obvious	69
Chapter 7:	Not Against Flesh and Blood	80
Chapter 8:	As It Was in the Days of Lot	100
Chapter 9:	A World Going Mad	111
Chapter 10:	Age of the Super Christian	121
Chapter 11:	It's Always Been Smoke and Mirrors	131
Chapter 12:	Christian, What Should You Do?	147
Chapter 13:	Behind Enemy Lines	164
Chapter 14:	Prayer Warfare	176
Chapter 15:	For the Non-Christian	184

For our struggle is not against flesh and blood, but against the rulers, against the powers, against the world forces of this darkness, against the spiritual forces of wickedness in the heavenly places.

– Ephesians 6:12 (NASB)

FOREWORD

Jesus referred to Satan as the "ruler of this world" in John 14:30 (see also John 12:31). Some translations use the word "prince" instead of "ruler," but the meaning is clear. For now, Satan controls what happens on this earth, yet it should go without saying (but I'll say it any way) that Satan can only do what God *allows* him to do--though it appears from Scripture that Satan often gets free reign to create as much terror and havoc as he needs.

When Jesus died and, due his sinless nature, rose from the dead three days later, Satan was not only put on notice, but his kingdom came under *judgment*. In fact, as commentator John Phillips points out, *"With the advent of Christ, Satan's kingdom on earth was put under siege."*[1]

That does not mean that Satan is overruled *now* in everyone's life. In fact, Satan still reigns in this world due solely to the fact that the world consists of *fallen people*, people who are literally called "sons of disobedience" (cf. Colossians 3:6; Ephesians 2:2; 5:6). The words of Paul are clear when he points out how authentic Christians used to walk in this world. He states, *"...in which you formerly walked according to the course of this world, according to the prince of the power of the air, of the **spirit that is now working in the sons of disobedience**"* (Ephesians 2:2; emphasis added). Notice that Paul is speaking in the present tense ("now working"). Wherever Satan finds an open door – and an open door exists in *every non-believer* – he uses it to further his kingdom.

However, we also need to recognize that during Jesus' time on earth and immediately following His death, resurrection, and ascension, He

---

[1] John Phillips, *Exploring the Gospel of John* (Grand Rapids MI Kregel Publications, 1989), 238

(through the Holy Spirit) began calling men and women to Himself to form His Bride. In essence then, God began to attack Satan's kingdom by calling people *out of that evil system* into God's Kingdom. Luke 10:19 tells us, *"Behold, I have given you authority to tread on serpents and scorpions, and over all the power of the enemy, and nothing will injure you."*

We must accept and appropriate this authority to use it in order to save people from the kingdom of Satan. If Jesus has given us the authority to overcome the enemy, then we need to use it to free the captive. Bear in mind that the overriding reason we enter the battle is for the salvation of souls. It's not to become bigheaded about that authority as the 70 did after they returned to Jesus. *"The seventy returned with joy, saying, 'Lord, even the demons are subject to us in Your name'"* (Luke 10:17). Note that Jesus responded to them by telling them that they should rather glory in the fact that their names were written in the book of Life!

In spite of Christ's victory, Satan is still temporarily allowed to be the immediate ruler of this world. Paul makes this point in his letter to the Ephesians several times. In Ephesians 2:1-2, Paul tells us that we *"...were dead in [our] trespasses and sins, in which [we] formerly walked according to the course of this world,* **according to the prince of the power of the air***, of the spirit that is now working in the* **sons of disobedience***."* (Emphasis added)

Satan continues to hold sway over the disobedient in this world. He moves kings, despots, dictators, and the average person to do his will. He rules the world from the air above it and he has hordes of demons doing his bidding. They live to serve him, bringing his goals to fruition.

Commentator William Hendriksen points out that *"God has tenanted the super mundane realm with innumerable hosts, and that in its lower region the minions of Satan are engaged in their destructive mis-*

sions."[2] Hendriksen, like others, goes on to note that the fallen spiritual entities are not the only ones who work in that realm. God's angelic servants do the same, supporting those of God's Kingdom.

In the previously quoted passage from Ephesians 2, it is important to realize that Paul references the fact that Satan "is now working." This is present tense. Satan continuously directs his energies to work in and through those people who are disobedient to God. In essence then, Paul says that those who do not *believe* are the disobedient ones, and because they do not believe in the gospel of Truth, Satan holds sway over them. They are his puppets to use for his purposes for as long as they remain in his kingdom of darkness.

Later in Ephesians, Paul teaches that we do not wrestle against flesh and blood (cf. Ephesians 6:12). In fact, the implication here is that it would be better if this was the case because of exactly how mortal and frail (comparatively speaking) humanity is when compared to demons, devils, and fallen angels. Our real war is against those spiritual beings in the heavenly realms. This is a fact which we must acknowledge.

Hendriksen again notes that "*as those who – under the permissive providence of God – are in tyrannical control of the world of ignorance, sin, and sadness; and as 'the spiritual forces of evil* in the heavenly places,' *that is, in the super mundane realm.*"[3]

In his second letter to the Corinthians, Paul refers again to Satan and his warfare against this world and God's Kingdom. He says, "*in whose case the* **god of this world has blinded the minds of the unbelieving** *so that they might not see the light of the gospel of the glory of Christ, who is the image of God*" (2 Corinthians 4:4; emphasis added). Here, Paul calls Satan the *god of this world*. As this world's god, he blinds

---

[2] William Hendriksen *Galatians, Ephesians, Philippians, Colossians, and Philemon* (Grand Rapids MI, Baker, 1968), 114
[3] Ibid, 272

people to the truth regarding the gospel of Jesus Christ. He does it in a plethora of ways, using rock music, the emergent church, the occult, politics, ever-changing societal norms, and too many other things to name in this book.

We know that Satan controls much within the spiritual dimensions and we will show that in this book. This is *not* to say or somehow imply that God is powerless, of course, as this is not true. It simply means that Satan's control of what takes place on earth often *begins* in the spiritual realms that we cannot see. Do we need to look any further than the book of Job to gain such insight?

It is clear that Satan created tornados and placed the desire in neighboring marauding armies to take what Job had, whether it was his family or his herds. These natural and physical attacks came out of nowhere. Job certainly failed to see them coming. He only saw the *results* of their attacks, and though it must have devastated him, he remained faithful to God throughout.

Satan has obviously set up his own servants to watch over certain areas of this world that is under his control so that they can hamper God's work, stifle the prayers of His saints, and so Satan can essentially insert himself into the affairs of mankind throughout the globe. We see the results of this globally and as Christians, we must stand against Satan and those of his kingdom.

We see evidence of satanic assault in the life of Jesus. We see it in the life of Paul. Though Satan's attack often came through unbelievers, we must remember that the attack always *starts* with Satan or one of his demonic underlings.

We need to realize that once a person *becomes* an authentic Christian, he or she remains on this earth as a combatant in *enemy territory*. Like a marine dropped just inside the enemy zone, our task is to engage the enemy and pull people from enemy territory.

Prior to our conversion to Christianity, we were no threat to Satan because in principle we agreed with him, whether we thought so or not. However, once we become true Christians, we find ourselves behind enemy lines. We are in enemy territory and neither Satan nor his minions look at us fondly. In fact, we are told that we are hated. *"If the world hates you, you know that it has hated Me before it hated you. If you were of the world, the world would love its own; but because you are not of the world, but I chose you out of the world, because of this the world hates you"* (John 15:18-19). For the remainder of our lives, we remain in enemy territory and must fight against the powers of darkness. To do what, change the world? No. Our fight is found in the spread of the gospel of Jesus Christ. Satan will resist our efforts, but the victory is ours in Christ.

This is what Jesus did and it was what Paul did, along with many other individuals noted in the New Testament. They fought the enemy of our souls by continuing to advance the gospel of Jesus so that those who are disobedient can have the opportunity to become authentic followers of Him who died for us.

We should not be fighting to somehow fix this world. We should be fighting for the very souls that Satan wants to destroy, and we were at one time among them. That is what the fight is all about, not who becomes president of the United States or how we can allegedly fix the ills of the world through legislation. While we can and should exercise our privilege to vote for what we know is right, we need to understand that none of these other things can or should remove us from the path that seeks to advance the gospel message.

It can be very easy to become embroiled in rallying for a political candidate that we believe will change our part of the world for the better. If we have opportunity to do that, then we should. However, if it becomes obvious that our political aspirations are pushing the desire to see the lost saved off to the side, then something is tragically wrong. Our number one mission in life is to witness to the lost and to see the disobedient become *obedient*. This will only happen when people become *authentic* Christians. It will not happen by trying to rebuild what Satan is in the process of destroying: the physical and geo-political world and its mindset.

One day, this world will be destroyed – but not by humanity or the devil. The Bible tells us that God Himself will destroy this world, replacing it with a new earth and new heavens to match. For now, Satan rules the roost, bringing forth as much evil as society allows, continuing to blind the hearts and minds of those who refuse to even acknowledge that truth apart from what they believe could exist.

Because of Satan's influence, evil not only marches onward but grows at an unprecedented rate today. If not for the restraining power of the Holy Spirit (primarily through the *invisible* Church), the demonic hordes would hold full sway over God's Creation.

Because of Satan's control and power, this world is quickly marching toward a one-world government. We can bank on that because it is prophesied in God's Word (Daniel 7:23-24; see also Revelation 13), and Satan is the one who will make it happen. To understand and accept this is *not* fatalism. It is simply t recognizing the truth of God's Word as well as God's higher purposes for humanity and all of His entire Creation.

So with respect to this coming coalescence of all current countries into something uniformly *one*, what should the Christian's response be? There are many who are running around like chickens with their heads removed telling people that if America will repent and turn to God, we as a nation might still be saved. On the other side, there are also plenty who are content to ignore what is happening.

Others have fallen into the trap of fighting against the perceived enemy, Islam, believing that halting the encroachment of Islam means the salvation of our democracy. At one time, I tended to believe that same thing, and it is easy to get caught up in the patriotic emotionalism the situation tends to create.

But what if doing these things means working *against* God? What if that is *not* what He wants His children to be involved in? What *then*? What if in fighting *against* Islam, we lose sight of the fact that God wants us to preach the gospel to those *within* Islam? It is difficult to do both, and as tensions run very high today, it is easy to become caught up in the former while completely ignoring the latter.

It is way too easy to forget what Paul tells us: that we are *not* in a war against other people (flesh and blood), though it may certainly seem as though we are up to our necks in it. We are actually warring against principalities and powers whose home is the invisible realm of spiritual dimensions beyond our eyesight. Paul makes this clear to us in his letter to the Ephesian believers (Ephesians 6:12).

Knowing that we are waging a battle against *unseen* (and in most cases, *unknown*) forces changes the tone of things, or *should*. It is easy to walk the family dog in a neighborhood at night and to be alert while doing so because one never knows when a mugging might occur. Being alert helps us to avoid these problems. This type of threat is always a potential because we never know when a criminal or thug might pop up, and it is usually when we least expect it that it happens. But even if/when that does happen, if we are somewhat prepared for the eventuality, we can do our best to either avoid the situation altogether or fight our way out of it.

There are certain areas of a city where I will not go after dark. Some of them are not even good enough to walk through during the day, and to do so is to invite the opportunity to become a victim. To avoid being the victim, I do what I can to avoid being where criminal activity takes place.

With *visible* thugs, we can see what is coming if we are alert and are fighting a flesh and blood opponent. However, when the enemy is *invisible*, something far more than brawn and alertness is required. An invisible enemy requires *faith* – faith in God and His ability to overcome.

I fully believe that the Bible tells us of these unseen enemies, those who prefer the anonymity of other spiritual dimensions and who come to our physical dimension donning the cloak of invisibility. This allows them to wreak unknown havoc on our systems of government, money, and society as a whole. An unseen enemy is extremely difficult to deal with, yet this is the Christian's calling. It goes with the territory of being a Christian.

This book is about the *Bible* and the *future*. There is information in the Bible that provides us with knowledge of truth about these unseen forces. We learn not only what they do, but how they travel and how they arrive to our dimension. We learn that we are involved in an epic battle in which our enemy naturally exists in other dimensions, dimensions that we know very little about. Most importantly, we learn how all things will culminate from God's perspective.

I've written two books that detail a great deal of what these beings do (*Demons in Disguise* and *Nephilim Nightmare*), their origins, how they work, and their final disposition. This book is about the true dangers they possess against all of humanity, yet we will find that we are not without hope in God. This book is called *Behind Enemy Lines* for a reason. It highlights not only that these invisible, malevolent enemies of our souls travel back and forth from their dimension to ours and reveals what they have worked to accomplish for millennia, but we learn what God's overriding purposes have always been.

The purpose of this book is not to incite fear, but to engender a strong sense of responsibility within the authentic Christian. What should our response to their presence be? Can we *fight* them?

Should we fight them, or would doing so simply take us from the path that God has us on?

In spite of all of their mortal and malevolent activity, what God is doing and why He keeps His Bride here is the most important question this book will answer. While it seems as though these invisible enemies have free reign in society and throughout the world to do whatever they wish to do, in truth, they don't. The plain fact of the matter is that God has *never* abandoned His throne or His people and never will. He watches everything that occurs on this earth and throughout His Creation as carefully now as He did when He first created everything.

Knowledge is power, and the more we know *from* God's Word about what these invisible agents of Satan are attempting to accomplish, the better we will be able to war against them, *spiritually*.

The great divide is coming and is very likely here. All authentic Christians need to realize which side they are on and need to work to bring God's saving grace to the lost people of this world. We cannot be overwhelmed or sidetracked by what we do not understand. We must press on, one by one, introducing people to the only Person who can actually make a difference in their lives.

Thank you for reading this book. I pray that because of it, you will gain a greater desire to see people come to the Lord. The time is short. Take up your cross and follow Him into the fields that are ripe for harvest.

Fred DeRuvo, August, 2012

Chapter 1
The Prince of Persia

I n the book of Daniel, chapter ten, we read the following words: *"But the prince of the kingdom of Persia was withstanding me for twenty-one days; then behold, Michael, one of the chief princes, came to help me, for I had been left there with the kings of Persia"* (Daniel 10:13).

That situation may not seem so odd to people, that one powerful demon (prince of the kingdom of Persia) could war against one of the angels from God's camp, keeping him at bay. After all, this is what takes place within the spiritual realm: spiritual battle.

What *is* a bit strange is what this same angel tells Daniel after he has finished explained the meaning of one of the visions Daniel has had. He says, *"But I shall now return to fight against the prince of Persia; so I am going forth, and behold, the prince of Greece is about to come"* (Daniel 10:20b).

Here's my question: why did this angel from God have to go back to the throne the same way he arrived to Daniel? We know that in order for that angel to arrive to Daniel, he spent 21 days fighting against the prince of Persia. Because we are dealing with an angel from the Lord, we automatically know that this was occurring in the spiritual realm, so we can rule out the fact that he was fighting against human beings. The angel from God was obviously and clearly fighting against the powers and principalities in the heavenly realms (cf. Ephesians 6:12) that Paul warned us about, and strong ones at that!

If you were walking home one night and there appeared in front of you a gang of thugs, would you not find a more circuitous route that would lead you back home instead of trying to fight your way through that gang? Moreover, if you managed to fight your way past the gang initially, when you left to go somewhere else, would you go back the same way or would you try to find a route that did not include running the gauntlet through that gang again?

Apparently, what we have in these two sections of Daniel 10 shows us something very important. Whoever the angel was that initially arrived to reveal the message of the vision (most conservative commentators believe it was Gabriel), we know that he was waylaid by the prince of Persia and was literally kept from continuing on his journey to reach Daniel. This tells us a couple of things that are extremely important:

1. Not all angels (fallen/unfallen) are equal in strength; some are more powerful than others
2. There was a specific route that the angel had to take to reach Daniel because of Daniel's location in the physical world

When I was much younger in my faith, I tended to think of the spiritual realm as merely being the sky above me. I assumed when angels needed to move from one part to the other they simply sped invisibly through the open space much like Superman does in the cartoons. Superman did not follow a flight plan. He simply pointed himself in the direction he needed to go and went there, as the crow flies.

Birds do this all the time. They might be perched on a branch of a tree and then something catches their eye, so off they go in that new direction, in a fairly straight path. I assumed that angels did the same thing. When they needed to get from God's throne or some other portion of heaven to a place on the earth, they simply took a direct path to get there. There was no fuss or muss. We all know that the quickest route from one point to the next is a straight line.

But here in Daniel 10 we note a problem. The angel had to go *through* a particular territory that was controlled in this case by a being the Bible refers to as the "prince of Persia." Persia in those days is Iran today, and it seems clear that this particular prince or spiritual demon had control of the comings and goings of other spiritual beings through that region. He protected it according to his desires and wishes.

Why did the angel that God sent need to travel through that location? Why not find another route to take? Maybe there was none. Maybe that was the gate that led from God's throne to the location of Daniel.

Some might say that the angel could have simply been unexpectedly overtaken by the prince of Persia as the prince saw the angel attempting to traverse the dimension. He likely knew where God's angel was heading and set out to stop him. He was successful for three weeks until Michael arrived and fought against the prince of Persia, allowing the original angel to continue on his way and carry out his mission, bringing the answer from God's throne to the prophet Daniel. Maybe it was all accidental. We might be tempted to think that except for what this same angel tells Daniel in verse twenty of Daniel ten.

In that verse, the angel makes it clear that he needs to go back the same way by which he came *to* see Daniel. He notes that he needed to go back to fight the prince of Persia again, but he also lets us know of another prince, the prince of Greece, who is "*about to come.*"

I gain a few insightful bits of information from this brief dialogue between the angel and Daniel.

1. There are powerful spiritual beings controlling areas of this world and they are in place by Satan's orders
2. There are specific portals or gates through which God's angels must pass to gain access to this world from God's throne

This is fascinating to me because it provides a glimpse into the entire area of the inter-dimensional world that thrives all around us, yet, in the normal course of life, we are powerless to see. The way in which angels come into and leave this physical realm is one thing. We really don't know much about the process. More important is what these beings attempt to do once they gain *access* to this physical world.

Of far more importance is the reality that these spiritual beings – the fallen ones – control a great deal of what goes on in this world, but they are rarely, if ever, seen. What we see instead are the individual human beings they have chosen to work in and through. In fact, I believe many of these extremely powerful *human* beings that are controlled by these malevolent forces are *never* seen. They are so far in the background that it is very likely the world will never see their faces until such a time as the world becomes thoroughly one in government and in purpose. The people we see now as being very powerful are likely little more than puppets themselves, fully deluded.

The real *human* powerbrokers, who have given themselves completely over to Satan and his purposes, remain deeply in the shadows, at least for the time being, until such a time as it becomes safe enough for them to reveal themselves to the world. This makes Paul's words of Ephesians 6:12 even more important. We do not fight against flesh and blood, but against the rulers in heavenly places who *use* certain human beings to get the job done. One can only guess as to what these people have been promised by these otherworldly beings. Chances are good that they are wealthy beyond measure. It would not surprise me to learn that some of the people who pull the strings have more money than some countries and they use their wealth not only to insulate themselves from others, but to create the type of havoc and upheaval we are currently seeing and experiencing throughout the world today.

We will spend a bit of time learning about the way the spiritual beings travel to and fro from their world to ours. The truth of the matter is that we must never lose sight of what God is doing and that He has absolute sovereignty over all of His Creation. This includes the fallen angels who, along with Satan, have endeavored to overthrow God's rule from the moment they fell.

If we focus on individual human beings, we will become entangled and enmeshed in something that is far bigger than we can ever imagine. In doing so, we will become lost to the reality of what God is doing because our focus will no longer be on Him, but on mere people.

Satan wants us to focus our time and attention on people, people like George Soros, or Mr. Obama, or other politicians and powerful leaders who seem to be working hard to overthrow the democratic nature of this country. I believe when we start focusing on people, we *cease* to realize that the powers and principalities have engaged us. This is exactly what those powers want us to do because they know that once we cease to focus our attention on the war we have with *them*, it quickly becomes as though we are trying to stick our fingers in this hole or that hole, attempting to plug the many breeches we know exist in the dam. The focus needs to be on the actual war in the heavenlies that occurs on a daily basis and its purpose. It is there that the battles are fought, lost or won. Ultimately, God is Victor and allows us to share in that victory as we abide in Him (cf. John 15).

As authentic Christians, we have an obligation to fight the good fight, and that does not mean standing up against human beings as if *they* are the enemy. Clearly, many people today are being *used* by these powers and principalities in spiritual places just as Judas Iscariot was, but in the end, these people *need Jesus*. They need salvation and they must be given the opportunity to hear the gospel message. Sometimes that is done with words. However, it should *always* be done with our *lives*.

The spiritual powers and principalities that exist and war against the saints of God and His Creation will *never* be saved. They know the gospel message and they realize its truth, but they will never have the opportunity to be forgiven or to receive the salvation from the Lord. It is a biblical impossibility because of the decision they made to follow Satan.

In their hatred of God and His Creation, they willingly use people to accomplish their goals for this planet. We see this throughout the world and we stand back in horror wondering how human beings can do such terrible things to one another. Humans are fully culpable for their atrocious acts, yet it must be understood that behind the people and their heinous acts stand overlords, powers, principalities, and a legion of demonic hosts prompting the lost of this world to traffic in the very things that Satan provides in the hopes of destroying this world as we know it and overcoming God Himself.

It is always interesting to me to see how God allows things to come into play. He allows the upheaval that is taking place in this world. He allows the criminal element to gain a stronger foothold. God allows people to become racists and be filled with hatred because they choose to ignore God and want nothing to do with Him. God allows all manner of sexual perversion and sin to become the norm in society. But there will be a day of reckoning.

That people want to overthrow America and other democratic-leaning countries is clear, and God permits it because He has a far larger agenda that needs to come to fruition. It is easy to see these things taking place throughout America and the world and to feel forlorn or hopeless.

Whether it's political unrest or societal ills, we want to believe that this country – the United States of America – was founded on Christian principles and that because of that, through solid effort, righteousness, and sheer might we can regain what has been lost. Can we? Is that what the Bible says?

Are we to be heavily involved in making a political difference in the lives of people? Should we throw down the gauntlet and take up the sword of righteousness against all the ills in society?

I am inclined to believe that while we have a responsibility to vote and stand up for what is right, the greatest thing we can do is fight for the lives of those who do not yet know Jesus. We can kid ourselves into thinking that if we can "straighten out America," all will be well with the world. The truth of the matter is that even if that *were* possible, we would only be arriving to the false conclusion that if America were turned around, so would the lives of people who live here be. It doesn't work that way.

People need the Lord. They need His salvation. That is the most important thing that we can ever hope to realize and attempt to achieve. We will not be rewarded for how politically involved we were in this life. God will take no notice of how many people we got registered to vote or whether or not our efforts politically made a difference. The only thing that will matter is how we lived *for* Christ and whether or not we introduced anyone to Him at all!

Chapter 2
Stargates in the Sky

They would like us to believe it's all just harmless science fiction. They don't want us to really accept as true that these things could exist. At the same time, according to the Bible, these things *do* exist and they are used to allow spiritual beings – both fallen *and* unfallen – to gain access to this world and the people living here.

The television *Stargate* series was a science fiction series of shows that began with the movie of the same name. The basic concept is that there are gates or portals allowing people and aliens to travel from one planet or galaxy to another in the blink of an eye. The Stargate could be closed and locked down to keep unwanted beings out. Though it was normally used for relatively good purposes in the movie and series, it was also clearly used by the bad guys to gain access to places where they could create problems.

In the *Stargate Atlantis* series, the main nemeses are the *Wraith*, interestingly enough. They are tall and lean and have blue skin, whitish hair, eyes with slits, and fangs. They eat humans. They're formidable, dangerous, and everyone who values life tries their best to stay away from them unless they have enough fire power to handle them.

The long-awaited movie *The Avengers* was released to the public and became an instant hit. Based on Marvel characters – Ironman, Thor, the Hulk, Black Widow, Captain America, and others – the movie showed these individuals coming together as the Avengers to fight against an enemy from another star system. This group is called to wage war against Thor's brother Loki, who has made a bargain with an alien group known as Chitauri. Interestingly enough, with their six fingers and other anomalies these beings could have been taken from a page of classical Greek writings.

The plot of the movie involves the Chitauri opening a portal (or Stargate) that allows them passage from their galaxy to ours. Through the power, might, and cooperation of the Avengers, the Chitauri are defeated and the portal is closed. Of course, the end of the movie hints at another enemy that will eventually focus its attention on earth and the earthlings.

It's almost as if science fiction shows like the *Avengers* and the *Stargate* franchise have taken a page from biblical history. The amazing part is that in many ways, I believe what we see in these shows has elements of truth to it, while at the same time it is presented in a way that is sure to be seen as merely science fiction. In other words, it's a way for the demonic realm to hide in plain sight by telling humans what their world is like, yet presenting it in such a way that it will simply be seen as entertainment and little more.

At the same time, people are enamored with what is viewed as science fiction these days. They *want* to believe that Stargates or some other inter-dimensional doorways exist today that connect one world or galaxy with another. They really like the idea, and because of that they tend to want to open themselves up to these things.

Besides the Avengers and the Stargate series, there are plenty of science fiction dramas and episodic television series that portray people with special attributes and even godlike abilities. Shows such as *Warehouse 13* focus on "artifacts" that need to be "snagged, tagged, and bagged" by special government agents who are constantly on the lookout for items that could potentially create havoc throughout the world. These items take control over people and nature, giving the holder of said item the ability to shape their world while doing great harm – knowingly or unknowingly – to others around them.

Taken by themselves, these shows are simply modern-day escapist fare with highly defined special effects that add to the believability. But how many people in the world today believe to some extent that scenarios and individuals like those in these shows could exist in real life?

Other shows like *Alphas* focus on human beings who are superheroes. *"The series follows a group of people with superhuman abilities, known as 'Alphas', as they work to prevent crimes committed by other Alphas.*[4] Who does not want to have superhuman abilities, either to prevent crime or get away with it? It is reminiscent of the TV show *Heroes,* which aired from 2006 to 2010. *"The series tells the stories of ordinary people who discover superhuman abilities, and how these*

---

[4] http://en.wikipedia.org/wiki/Alphas

abilities take effect in the characters' lives. The series emulates the aesthetic style and storytelling of American comic books, using short, multi-episode story arcs that build upon a larger, more encompassing arc."[5]

Within the past ten years or so, these types of shows have become normal TV fare. Fed a steady diet of science fiction, is it any wonder that viewers are enamored with and want more of these types of shows?

But one has to wonder why these shows have become so hot, so sought after and so religiously watched. It is all part of an underlying need and desire to brainwash the average person into thinking that these concepts – while still remaining in the realm of science fiction – are ultimately things to be craved.

On my blog[6], I have written about things such as astral projection and how believable and sought after it has become today. There are those who will attest to the fact that they personally use it for sexual satisfaction by becoming involved with beings they meet during astral projection episodes.

The amazing thing is how many people who purport to be Christians have written to me telling me that I have no clue about that which I speak. They boldly claim that astral projection for the Christian, while it has its dangers, is or should be the *norm*. They argue that there is nothing wrong with it and in fact, we learn a great deal from being involved in astral projection. Because of that, we should not deny its reality. It should be seen as simply another weapon in the Christian's spiritual arsenal to learn about God and our enemy.

While the Bible itself does not clearly come out and condemn such practices like astral projection, there are most certainly *guidelines* in

---

[5] http://en.wikipedia.org/wiki/Heroes_%28TV_series%29
[6] http://www.studygrowknowblog.com

Scripture that we should use to help us determine whether or not something is good or evil.

Three such references are the following:

- Deuteronomy 18:10,11
- Leviticus 19:31, and
- Isaiah 8:19,20

These and other verses speak of avoiding necromancy (conjuring up the dead), spiritism, and mediums. While it might be argued (as some have) that many enter into astral projection through no real effort on their part (in other words, it supposedly just happens), this is not an excuse and does not relinquish culpability in the situation.

As fallen human beings, we are cut off from certain spiritual dimensions, and God has done that for our own safety. Ever since the fall of humanity, God sealed off from us a number of dimensions that our first parents enjoyed. Because of the fall, we lost a great number of things, and likely included in that is the ability to go from dimension to dimension as spiritual beings do. Again, this is for our protection.

Paul says that we see through a glass darkly (cf. 1 Corinthians 13:12), but *then* we will see face to face. The word "then" means *after death*. Paul is speaking of what happens to us after we pass from this life to the next and the veil is removed because our sin nature will no longer be with us.

Yet we have a growing number of people who actively look for ways to astrally project themselves into other dimensions. If they aren't actively trying to accomplish this, they say they are simply caught up in it through no real choice of their own. Yet they don't actively *reject* the situation either, but willingly go along for the ride. This is because they prefer the *experience* of allegedly riding through the heavens rather than getting to know God through His Word. They deny this, but the truth speaks volumes.

Astral projection is simply another way to travel through dimensions, much like an open portal or Stargate. I have often wondered about these Stargates, or heavenly portals, that are referenced in Scripture. The situation in Daniel 10, as previously noted, is a case in point. It certainly seems as though the angel that came to Daniel providing him with the answer he sought was bound to meet the prince of Persia coming and going. It appears as though he did not have the chance to go another route, which may have helped him avoid this prince.

Look at the situation revolving around the Tower of Babel in Genesis 11. Many believe that Nimrod was a Nephilim. He was listed as a hunter of men. In all likelihood, Nimrod was a *type* of Antichrist, the first of his kind. He not only hunted for men, gathering them to himself as a hen gathers her chicks, but he was completely *opposed* to everything God was doing.

Nimrod led the people to build a tower. This tower was to reach the heavens. As numerous scholars have stated, the plan may not have been to reach what we consider to be the heavens so much as it was to reach a particular portal that was in existence that would have allowed these beings to find their way back into the heavenly realms. It's not far-fetched, and because we see the use of portals or gates in other areas of Scripture, the idea that Nephilim (somehow fathered by fallen angels and human women) had it in their DNA to want to get back to their "first estate" from where their fathers came becomes something worth considering.

But note here in Genesis 11 that God saw what Nimrod was attempting to do and decided to put a complete stop to it. He did so by confusing the language of men, creating different cultures and languages by which people would come together. This put an instant stop to the plans of Nimrod because he lost most of his workers as they grouped up by language and went their separate ways.

Now, if the purpose of Nimrod was to build a tower that would allow him and others to gain access to the heavenly realm through a portal that existed, then this tells us that portals do exist and they are somewhat fixed in position. However, one wonders whether or not doors can be created and opened by people who do things that are forbidden by God with respect to the occult.

I believe that as human beings open themselves up to that part of the fallen spiritual realm, they are opening doors that allow demons to gain access to them and through them, greater portions of the physical world. We have glimpses of it throughout Scripture, of course, but beyond that, what we know comes from the mouths of demonic entities that cannot be trusted because lying is their native language.

I've read any numbers of books, and you may have as well, highlighting how aliens have abducted people and opened them up to a world that is beyond our normal vision. Knowledge of these worlds would certainly tempt anyone to think more highly of themselves than they ought, especially if that someone is not a Christian in the first place.

One after another, these books outline how the spiritually creative process works for human beings in conjunction with their "alien" hosts. I believe these beings are working overtime to convince fallen humanity that what lies just beyond our eyesight is something so fantastic and other-worldly that to not experience it means missing the mysterious truth of the hidden universe.

In other words, the main thrust of these demonic hordes is above all things to deceive people into believing that by gaining the experience of soul travel, or simply opening doors/portals to the spiritual realm, the knowledge that many seek will be found. These demons use whatever they can to reel in unsuspecting human beings. They have little difficulty in crafting their message to the individual human being.

If someone believes himself to be a Christian, what he learns is overtly religious, even Christian-sounding. If he is not a Christian, but simply a New Age thinker, the message is carefully constructed to suit him and his expectations.

There has been so much going on within certain branches of Christendom that will make your head spin. Most know of "holy laughter," an experience that takes place during some form of worship service where those in the congregation simply start laughing uncontrollably. This is supposedly the sign that the Holy Spirit has come and anointed the crowd. But the question is, what good comes from it? Apart from laughing until your pants are wet, *nothing* good comes from it! I have seen videos of these types of services where people laugh so hard they fall out of their seats or they fall over and on top of one another. There is no propriety, and the most damning part of this is that there is absolutely *nothing* in Scripture that provides support for such experiences.

Lately, within aspects of the Charismatic movement there are those who say they are Christian who are actively seeking experiences through astral projection. In fact, a history of the Charismatic movement shows that these groups have willingly opened themselves up to all sorts of experiences and manifestations that are nothing short of New Age chicanery. Yet few see a problem with it, and when a person speaks out against it, that person is attacked as if they know nothing and have no clue.

People within the visible Church have grown in their fascination and amazement of the *experience*, which is heavily demonic. Within the Charismatic movement, there is something new regarding astral projection. People are beginning to speak of their experience of projecting their spiritual body via astral projection to the third heaven and back. People are being taught that because we are "in Christ" we have the actual ability to ascend into heaven, as spiritual teacher Patricia King explains. As can be imagined, people are eating this up.

Who does not want to go see what heaven is like? After all, didn't Paul speak of his own experience of being taken to the third heaven (cf. 2 Corinthians 12)? If Paul did it, why can't we? If the apostle John experienced it in Revelation 4, why can't we?

The truth of the matter is that for both Paul and John, they did not know if their experience was a vision or an out-of-body experience. Beyond this, God did this to these men for a very special purpose. It was to further the gospel and write more of God's Word. Since we have God's Word with us today, there is no need for us to chase after or even expect astral projection events to occur in our life.

What Christians often forget is that Satan is extremely capable of creating hallucinatory events and experiences that appear to be as real as life itself. What we do not see in these events are truths that reflect the truth of the Bible. What we see instead are things that tend to tickle people's ears, and because of that, we should have nothing to do with them.

With respect to Paul and John, in both cases, God initiated the experience. Someone might come along and say, *"Yes! That's what happens to me too. I'm minding my own business and then all of a sudden, I'm experiencing some form of astral projection!"*

These people who experience these things have no trouble telling everyone about them. They leave no detail out. I've had people tell me about their experiences where they saw Jesus in situations He would never have been involved in because of the sinful nature of those events, yet that does not seem to matter to those people. They believe that because the experience occurred in another dimension, somehow right and wrong are different or don't apply. So, if Jesus comes to them as a drunken homeless man, so be it. It's Jesus and He is there to teach them something. The problem is that Jesus would *never* have been drunk in this life, so why is it okay for Him to be drunk during some out-of-body experience in some other dimension? Sin is sin whether it's sin here on this earth or in the heavenly realms.

We have the record of Paul and John, who in both cases were not allowed to relay at least some of the things they heard or saw while experiencing what they experienced. Yet in contrast, we have Patricia King, who states in one of her videos that there is *"such an acceleration of people having heavenly encounters – access into the glory realm – and seeing things and experiencing things."*[7] However, if we look to Scripture, it becomes clear that these types of experiences may fall under something else entirely. Paul gives us a clue when he says, *"that is, the one whose coming is in accord with the activity of Satan, with all power and signs and false wonders"* (2 Thessalonians 2:9).

Here Paul clearly speaks of the future Antichrist, whose entrance onto the world's stage will be accompanied by *"power and signs and false wonders."* If we couple this with the fact that people are preferring to follow people who do nothing except tickle their ears with false doctrine that sounds inviting, we get the picture that maybe, just maybe, this world is falling under the spell of Satan himself as he preps for the final conflict between his man – the Antichrist – and God the Son. People will simply be his useful pawns in the game.

How else would we see so many New Age type experiences entering into the world of Christendom? It is becoming obvious that people today do *not* want sound doctrine. They want *experiences* because they believe they are often defined by these experiences. They want to participate in exciting events that make them feel important about themselves and the world in which they live.

What I also note about many of these people and ministries who focus on experience is that to hear them tell it, God is doing something

---

[7] http://www.youtube.com/watch?v=dKfFhM1W5R8 (April 21, 2012)

so remarkable and ecstatic that only the blind and dumb would not want to be part of it; yet what we see in Scripture is that God in Christ has told us just how bad things will get before He returns. Paul and Peter discuss the same thing.

Individuals like Patricia King, however, seem completely unaware of Jesus' words in Matthew 24, Mark 13, and Luke 21 (the Olivet Discourse). They speak as if things will progressively get better and then *voila!* God will return to reign supreme over the earth. Really? Is that how it will happen?

This is the goal of the fallen angels and their propaganda. They want the world to believe that through effort, work, and toil, the entire globe will become a better place for human beings to live and work. They want us to think that in spite of the upheaval, things are truly getting better and the world is ready to move to the next spiritual plane in the evolutionary process.

The lies that exist throughout society and that are being believed on a massive scale suggest something far more nefarious than simply human beings trying to accomplish something. What is occurring in and throughout global society is the result of powerful beings that know the score and know how to manipulate the masses to accomplish their ends.

We see this occurring throughout Christendom as well as the world at large. We see what the enemy is attempting to accomplish and it is not pretty, but we need to constantly compare that to what God is doing, not what we want to see happening. We must always remember that God is fully in control and that He will never change even though the things we see in society are not to our liking.

Chapter 3
Too Much Water Under the Bridge

According to the Bible, the world is *not* going to become better and better until Jesus is finally able to step up and take His rightful place as ruler of the world. There are movements afoot now that want to see America returned to its foundation, believing that the U.S., having been founded upon biblical principles, needs simply to return to that ideal and all will be well with America and, hence, the world. This is patently false. In fact, I fully believe it is too late and we have come too far for any return to what some might call normalcy. There is too much going on behind the spiritual scenes, and it is happening too fast to stop it or even keep it from moving forward. That may sound like a *defeatist* attitude, but the truth is that clear if only we will take the time to see it.

In this day and age, truth itself is under attack from all sides. In fact, in some countries, stating the truth about Islam (or homosexuality) can result in a fine, jail sentence, or even death. Biblical truth is pivotal and unchanging, and in some cases, the only way people can deny the truth is to make it against the law by trying to redefine it as "hate speech."

That doesn't mean we avoid telling the truth. It means we become aware of and take into consideration the potential consequences – and continue broadcasting the truth anyway!

When I write an article in my blog on astral projection, homosexuality, or something dealing with the New Age, I am amazed to see how many people will come out of the woodwork attempting to call me judgmental, critical, or simply way off base. Certainly, they're entitled to their opinions, but the reality is that they are attempting to shut me down by calling truth into question. They don't like what I have to say, and since it does not square with their *experience* and beliefs, silencing me is ultimately what they want to achieve. This is all part of that "tickling of the ears" that people have become so fond of today, and it will only worsen with time.

In general, people do not want to hear solid doctrine or theology. They don't want to be taught that there is one truth. Truth annoys them, so they don't want to hear it. They prefer to immerse themselves in teaching that makes them feel good, makes them believe that the world is moving toward a higher good, and provides them with an outlook that says life will only get better.

This is unmitigated hogwash! Who is anyone to denigrate what Jesus has clearly stated about what will happen during the end times, times in which I believe we are fully immersed? Jesus clearly demonstrated through His teaching that during the last days, life would become hell on earth. Just a quick glance at Matthew 24 proves this to be the case, yet today we have all sorts of preachers and teachers telling us an alternate, fairy tale future. They are quick to make light of Jesus' words by attempting to redirect people in thinking that what Jesus spoke of already happened and culminated in A.D. 70, or they allegorize His Words to mean something they do not mean. They prefer allegory over truth. In His Olivet Discourse of Matthew 24, Jesus clearly references the *entire* world as the context or backdrop of His teachings and dire warnings. He wasn't simply speaking about Jerusalem, though parts of His teachings do reference and include Jerusalem. He was speaking about the literal hell that will visit the entire globe during the end times, times which I and many others believe have arrived.

The entirety of Matthew 24 speaks of the horrors that will visit this planet during the time before the seven years of Tribulation. Do we honestly believe that this coming seven-year period of time has already occurred in the distant past, and that the Antichrist who Daniel in Daniel 7 and 9 says will rule the *entire* world has already come and gone?

The plain fact of the matter is that legions of demonic hosts are alive and well and doing their level best to occupy this world and deceive the people herein. That's their job and they take special delight in each soul they turn away and keep from God! This is what they do. Christians who get caught up in the political turmoil are doing no service to God because they are avoiding their true calling, which is to bear fruit and be involved in the Great Commission.

Everything that is occurring around us, whether it's political or socioeconomic in nature, should be the impetus for us to desire to see soul after soul come to the Lord for salvation. Instead, too many are caught up in trying to turn things around. They work hard for change in November. They want certain politicians out and others in. They want a return to the Bible and principles upon which this country was founded. They tend not to see the reality of lost souls because they are focused elsewhere.

It is not wrong to vote. It is not wrong to try to work to make areas of society a better place, but if that becomes our sole or main focus, we obviously have lost sight of the Great Commission, and that needs to be our main focus. It cannot take a back seat to anything.

Beyond politics, there is a tremendous and growing interest in UFOs, aliens, space truckers, portals, and the like. People are thoroughly interested in the subject of what lies *beyond* our physical realm. They are catapulted via curiosity to seek out every book and speaker who seems to know anything about these areas. Instead of wanting to know God better and live a life that pleases Him, as well as helping to snatch souls from the fire before it's too late, we are ensconced in studying the spirit world and learning what we can learn even when the source of that information is less than credible. The Bible only tells us so much. For many, that's not good enough.

When Paul was taken up the third heaven, there were things he could not talk about afterwards. It was simply not permissible. He noted that in this life we see things darkly. In other words, because of the unseen wall that separates our world from the spiritual realms, there is much that we are not privy to and much that cannot be seen or understood. In spite of that lack of knowledge, we should continue to move on fulfilling the Great Commission because after all, if Christians don't tell others about the truth of salvation, who *will*?

Instead, many within Christendom have become enamored with knowledge of the forbidden. We do whatever we can to find some way to peel back the curtain in order to obtain a greater vantage point. But for what purpose? Do we really need to know?

It is one thing to understand *how* the spiritual realm works. It is actually important to have at least a basic grasp of how the beings within that realm work and operate as revealed in Scripture. Knowing about that makes us more astute and clear-headed, something Peter calls being sober minded. In fact, in his first letter, Peter mentions being sober minded no less than three times!

"Therefore, prepare your minds for action, keep sober in spirit, fix your hope completely on the grace to be brought to you at the revelation of Jesus Christ" (1 Peter 1:13).

"The end of all things is near; therefore, be of sound judgment and sober spirit for the purpose of prayer" (1 Peter 4:7).

"Be of sober spirit, be on the alert. Your adversary, the devil, prowls around like a roaring lion, seeking someone to devour" (1 Peter 5:8).

Yet today, people are anything but sober minded! Paul speaks against this type of mindset in Ephesians 4:14 by stating, *"As a result, we are no longer to be children, tossed here and there by waves and carried about by every wind of doctrine, by the trickery of men, by craftiness in deceitful scheming."* Just prior to this verse, Paul speaks of what our walk in Christ *should* be, but for too many it is the exact opposite.

We should walk in the fullness of the Spirit, relying on the gifts He has provided so that His Body, the Church, will be built up into a living organism that brings praise to God. IF we do that, *then* ("as a result"), we would no longer be like children, thrown around by the newest, latest, and greatest teaching, which normally comes through *"the trickery of men"* and is fully enveloped in *"deceitful scheming."*

Not only are people interested in knowledge of the forbidden, but many to turn to ministries that appear to have all the answers. When you look at many of these ministries today, it is very obvious that they have amassed a good deal of wealth. It certainly seems as though God has blessed them because of their riches and their books and video sales. They are well known throughout the world and leaders of those ministries have become household names. Everyone knows them, whether they agree with their teachings or not. This seems to indicate to many that material wealth and success is the direct result of God's blessing, but it may have nothing to do with it.

The problem is that in today's day and age, the fact that these people amass such large followings can only be due to the fact that they are teaching something that itches and tickles the ears of those who follow them. This is exactly what Paul means when he says, "**For the time will come when they will not endure sound doctrine**; *but wanting to have their ears tickled, they will accumulate for themselves teachers in accordance to their own desires*" (2 Timothy 4:3; emphasis added).

Paul is stating clearly and without equivocation that there will come a time when by and large, people will *not* want to hear the truth! They will prefer lies that make them *feel good*. This is a true statement and it points to the time toward the end of this current age, a time I believe we are living in now.

More and more people do not want to discuss and deal with things that they view as being bad, sad, or depressing. There is so much negativism every day that people deal with – the economy, the housing situation, politics, etc. – that they really don't want to turn to the Bible and hear more of the things that they construe to also be negative.

This unwillingness to want to learn about how prophetic events are unfolding is due to the fact that many within Christendom have a wrong view of what God is doing. They simply fail to understand

God's purposes and what those purposes mean in the midst of the things that we face as Christians.

In other words, if we truly understood that God was calling people from this world to become part of His invisible Church, we would adopt a different perspective, which is none other than God's perspective. Instead, we adopt a human viewpoint that is, in most cases, adopted from the fallen creatures within the spiritual realm.

One author said the following words, which never rang more true than they do today:

> *"Like every age, our age will also come to a close. It is here we find one of the vital errors amongst Christians at the present time. They never think of this age of Gospel preaching and Gospel privilege as coming to an end. If one speaks to them about the end of the age, they think it means after the world is converted, and the passing away of the world itself. Peter has given us the witness that this would be one of the characteristics of the last days, when mockers shall come, saying 'Where is the promise of His coming? For from the day the fathers fell asleep all things continue as they were from the beginning of the creation.' This is what we find so much in our day. In spite of the horrible conditions in which this age has been plunged, and the confirmation of the predictions of the Bible relating to this age, the mass of professing Christians expect that things will continue, and that after the war the age will speedily improve. We have seen before how impossible this is, for the Bible teaches us that this age is an evil age, and there is not a single passage which promises an improvement. On the contrary, everything in the Word shows that as the age ends, and its real end comes, all the evil conditions present in this age come to a head and climax. We find therefore a great deal said in the Scriptures about the end of the age. The Lord Jesus speaks of it in His parables in Matthew xiii. He has given also a complete panorama*

of the age-ending in His great Olivet Discourse. There when we come to the Epistles we find that the Spirit of God through every writer gives a warning and a witness about the end of the age. All these warnings and witnesses do not tell us of a converted world, and a world which is won to righteousness, of nations who lay down their armaments and no longer make war; nor do these warnings and predictions speak of a triumph of the doctrine of Christ. They tell us the very opposite. They give warnings that the faith is going to be rejected, that delusions and errors are going to multiply, that nation is going to lift up sword against nation and kingdom against kingdom, that lawlessness and unrighteousness are going to increase, and that the age itself is going to end in a time of trouble such as the world has never seen before."[8]

The above words were written in 1918, following World War I. World War II was a few years off yet, and Israel's national independence was roughly thirty years in the future. We can go through nearly every generation and find writers who penned words such as these since the time of Jesus and the apostles. Theirs are the words of one who calls out from the top of the wall to the inhabitants of the walled-in city below, warning them of impending doom, in spite of what people want to hear and believe and are unable to see because of their vantage point.

Imagine being safely tucked away inside a walled city with the watchers on the wall keeping an eye on the horizon, noting the first sign of coming disaster. Their job was to warn people so that preparations could be made. It would have been folly for the citizens of that walled city to ignore the shouted warnings of those on guard; yet, this is what has happened in the past and continues to happen now.

---

[8] Arno C. Gabelein, *Studies in Prophecy* (Biola Book Room, Los Angeles, CA 1918), 15-16

People do not want to hear bad news. They prefer to believe that things will get better, in spite of all evidence to the contrary. The Christian who turns his/her back on God's Word because it is none too comforting has effectively turned his/her back on God. I'm *not* saying that salvation is lost. I'm simply saying that those authentic Christians who prefer to fill their heads with spiritual tripe in order to feel good about themselves and their lives wind up rebelling against God, who has told us the truth about this age.

It is extremely difficult to stay on top of everything that happens in this world because it all happens so fast. In fact, it is likely impossible, but what we are able to learn is enough to make our heads spin with confusion and depression. That is, *if* we are unwilling to take God's Word seriously and truthfully.

Chapter 4
The Overarching Problem

Anywhere you look today you will see it – *if* you take the time to notice it. Evil is unfolding right before our eyes and yet there are those who believe they can stand against it and even turn back the tide! I say that it cannot be done because the Bible teaches that it *won't* be done by human beings. Too much that was once hidden and deliberately kept under cover is now out in the open.

Look at the condition of rock music today. It has come a very long way from the shake, rattle, and roll days of yesteryear, but those were the *early* stages, when the doors were first being forced open. Looking back on those very early days of rock and roll, it seems so innocuous now compared to what exists today. We might even be tempted to think that if only we had those good ol' days again, things would be better. But even then parents *during that day and age* were upset with people like Elvis Presley and groups like the Beatles. They not only represented something new, but they represented a movement *away* from the accepted norms of society, and not in a good way.

Elvis' pelvis was a shocker to many, and yet I'm convinced he was not intentionally trying to replicate a "sex" act on the stage as much as it was simply the way he danced. It didn't matter, though, because I believe he was used by powers and principalities to force open the door, allowing even more heinous things to eventually come through, things that we have and that are accepted as the norm today.

Consider the state of rock music today. I could name band after band that appears to have focused on demonism, but let's just focus on one: *Avenged Sevenfold*. This group is made up of young men who were raised in the Roman Catholic Church. They look gothic and are covered in tattoos and piercings. Their music is reflective of groups like *Metallica* with their driving beat and dark lyrics, and yet parts of their songs are very melodic and even easy on the ears.

Because of their religious background and training, many of their songs contain lyrics that have clear religious underpinnings and overtones. Take for example the lyrics to the song "Nightmare":

> *Dragged ya down below, down to the devils show,*
> *To be his guest forever (Peace of mind is less than never!)*
> *Hate to twist your mind, but God ain't on your side,*
> *An old acquaintance severed (burn the world your last endeavor!)*

Behind Enemy Lines

Flesh is burning, you can smell it in the air,
Cause men like you have such an easy soul to steal (steal)
So stand in line while they ink numbers in your head,
You're now a slave until the end of time here,
Nothing stops the madness turning, haunting, yearning,
pull the trigger!

You should have known the price of evil,
And it hurts to know that you belong here, yeah
Oooooh, it's your f**kin' nightmare!
(While your nightmare comes to life)

Can't wake up in sweat, cause it ain't over yet,
Still dancin' with your demons (Victim of your own creation)
Beyond the will to fight, where all that's wrong is right
Where hate don't need a reason (loathing self-assassination)

You've been lied to just to rape you of your site [sic],
and now they have the nerve to tell you how to feel (feel)
So sedated as they medicate your brain
and while you slowly go insane they tell ya:
Given with the best intentions help you with your complications!

You should have known the price of evil,
And it hurts to know that you belong here, yeah.
No one to call, everybody to fear,
Your tragic fate is looking so clear, yeah.
Oooooh, it's your f**kin' nightmare, ha-ha-ha-ha!

Fight (fight), not to fail (fail), not to fall (fall)
Or you'll end up like the others.
Die (die), die again (die), drenched in sin (sin)
With no respect for another.

Down (down), feel the fire (fire), feel the hate (hate)
Your pain is what we desire.
Lost (lost), hit the wall (wall), watch you crawl (crawl)
Such a replaceable liar.

And I know you hear their voices (calling from above),
And I know they may seem real (these signals of love),
But our life's made up from choices (some without appeal),
They took for granted your soul, and it's ours now to steal
(As your nightmare comes to life!)

You should have known the price of evil,
And it hurts to know that you belong here, yeah.
No one to call, everybody to fear,
Your tragic fate is looking so clear, yeah
Oooooh, it's your f**king nightmare!

Avenged Sevenfold has many songs that include the types of imagery noted in the above lyrics. If you watch videos of their live performances, you will hear the use of the "F-bomb" often as the lead singer talks to the gathered crowd, bantering back and forth or introducing the next song. While there have been a number of personnel changes over the years, their original drummer died a while ago due in part to a drug overdose. Now when they sing the song "Afterlife," they reference him (Jimmy "The Rev" Sullivan) as being in heaven. There is just something pervasively evil with many rock groups today, yet their persona is commonly accepted as the norm by many young people.

Here is a *partial* list of song titles from *Avenged Sevenfold*:

- A Little Piece of Heaven
- Afterlife
- Bat Country
- Beast and the Harlot
- Betrayed
- Darkness Surrounding
- We Come Out at Night
- The Wicked End
- Scream

Behind Enemy Lines

- Dear God
- Demons
- Dancing Dead
- God Hates Us
- To End the Rapture
- Eternal Rest

Some of the album names go like this:

- Sounding the Seventh Trumpet
- Walking the Fallen
- City of Evil

Here are the lyrics to their song *God Hates Us*:

Total Nightmare!
Total Nightmare!

You wanna hear my side?
You need to drown to know
With all the times,
It hurt me to f**k you,
I built a wall with your blood to show!

God Save Us!
God Save Us All!
God Hates Us!
God Hates Us All!
Total Nightmare!
Total Nightmare!

Nothing to heal
No one to break
Pills had a role now there's nothing to take
Nothing to trust
No one to fake!
You'll find out sooner that it's best if we just know our place!

Behind Enemy Lines

My infiltrated mind!
My lacerated soul
It took me years, create me, control you
I left myself for an idea I stole!

God Save Us!
God Save Us All!
God Hates Us!
God Hates Us All!
Total Nightmare!
Total Nightmare!

Liar Rape kill, Love Hate Fear

You better take your time
You better take it slow
Cuz when you seek the one
There's Nothing left to show

Total Nightmare!
Total Nightmare!

The words to *God Hates Us* could have been written by Satan himself, twisting the truth to make himself look good. Imagine any band producing songs with lyrics like these just ten or twenty years ago. Had that type of band existed, they would have been on the far fringe and deeply underground, certainly not solidly entrenched in the mainstream. Yet here we are in 2012, and this is only *one* band with lyrics that seem penned by a demon from hell. Worse, these are the lyrics that kids listen to and sing for their own enjoyment and listening pleasure!

In a recent video recording of *Avenged Sevenfold* live in concert in Germany at an event called *Rock Ring*, whether or not the concert goers in the crowd spoke English is unclear, but it was very obvious that they knew the words to the band's songs and sang along with each song. This says something drastic about the core group of young people today who look to bands like this for meaning and direction in life.

Now, I'm certainly *not* saying that the band members themselves worship Satan, and they just as likely may have no real clue as to how their songs and lyrics are being used by the enemy to spread his (Satan's) message of evil. In fact, it is clear that they believe, as they do about their recently deceased drummer, they will be in heaven one day. I fully believe that the enemy of our souls is using groups like *Avenged Sevenfold* to spread a message that becomes part of the worldview of millions of young people the world over, people who don't necessarily think for themselves, but take what is spoon fed to them in the form of songs and videos. Those things become the *doctrine* they believe and emulate.

The tragedy is that these are the types of groups that many young people will continue to look to for direction today to help frame their social conscience and awareness. The previously mentioned video of *Avenged Sevenfold's* live performance in Germany shows literally a sea of unending people at the concert, thousands upon thousands, all of them jazzed and excited to be there.

The terrible reality may be that groups like this, while not directly adoring and promoting worship of Satan, are doing something just as bad. In many instances, they may be speaking against what they believe to be the fallacies and/or hypocrisy they see within Christianity. Unfortunately for them, what they are actually seeing is what exists within *Christendom* as a whole, but not necessarily within *Christianity*, the former comprised of the visible and invisible Church, with the latter comprised only of the invisible Church.

Satanists see these groups as speaking out against what they believe to be the dead religion of Christianity. They believe that Satan has been around a good deal longer than Jesus and will outlast Christianity as well. Of course, it goes without saying that they ignore or deny the truth of Scripture when it states that Jesus was before all things and that through Him and by Him all things were created (cf. Colossians 1:15-18). Satanists believe that *Satan* created all things and that because of that he will eventually be enthroned physically, with their help. While they believe they do not worship him as we worship God in Christ, they believe that Satan has *freed* them from the chains of darkness that stemmed from the teachings of the Bible. Biblical truth is antiquated to them and because they believe the Bible to be false, they need to separate from it. This, they believe, is what Satan has helped them accomplish through the acquisition of secret *gnosis,* and while they do not believe that Satan wants or needs their worship, they have the utmost respect for him because of what they believe he has done *for* them.

Folks, we are arriving to a point where turning back the clock or forcing the closure of opened doors may be too late. Satan is using Satanists and music groups like *Avenged Sevenfold* to open the doors wider to what young people will accept today and to what will ultimately become their *standard*. When I see their videos, my heart goes out to these young men and to those who listen to their music because they are desperately lost, and the band is leading a generation of young people down the path toward eternal destruction.

Though they may not worship Satan directly, the members of *Avenged Sevenfold* look the part of the Satanic host. On stage, they sport bat tattoos and piercings, and bats and skulls are a big part of the show, along with fire shooting from towers parked near the back of the stage near their new drummer. A large graphic reproduction of one of their album covers stands behind the drummer. On it, we see Death, gravestones, and a person going down into the grave.

Satan has fully covered his bases. *Avenged Sevenfold* is merely one band among many that are doing his bidding, though I believe unknowingly. They are deceived into thinking that they know the truth about heaven and hell and they can create a mix of music that *seems* religious and even thought-provoking, yet it winds up literally preaching to untold millions of young people the world over and planting within them the lies that the enemy has included in the lyrics provided to the writers of *Avenged Sevenfold* songs.

From where do these songs and lyrics come? The members of *Led Zepplin* will tell you that their signature song from decades ago, "Stairway to Heaven," simply *came* to them one day. They didn't agonize over it and go through multiple writes and re-writes until they got it right. Words simply came to them like a gift out of the blue and very little work needed to be done on the song, which became an instant hit.

We think of youth today and wonder how many of them are *unchurched*, yet the reality seems to be that though they are un-churched, Satan has them exactly where he wants them: in a church of his own making. They stand opposed to God in this world and currently do not have salvation. Satan delights in the fact that so many young people today have no clue about him and have untrue ideas about heaven and hell.

For the young people of today who avidly listen to music by *Avenged Sevenfold* and a plethora of other rock groups of that and other genres, that is their church, and the stage is the pulpit. What they hear from that stage is the *doctrine* they come to know, believe, and live. Songs are extremely powerful forms of art. Have you wondered how a particular song got stuck in your head? You find yourself hearing it repeatedly and it becomes annoying, yet it's almost as if it needs to run its course or be actively replaced with something else before it will go away. Songs are very powerful, and most people can memorize a song very easily because it is accompanied by music, as opposed to simply memorizing text all by itself. These songs get deep into a person's heart and psyche and begin to direct the way that person thinks, talks, and lives.

Satan is getting through to all segments of society including aspects of the *visible* Church. He is leaving no stone untouched or unturned because he knows his time is short and his message of hell and hatred needs to get out there. Too many unthinking and critically unsound young people of today are swallowing the message, whether it's "preached" by groups like *Avenged Sevenfold* (their name taken from the Cain and Abel saga in Genesis in which God says He will avenge Cain's blood sevenfold) or some Marxist, Communist, or Socialist (termed "progressives" in today's vernacular) political leader who is too "cool" or charismatic to ignore. It is happening throughout the globe at an astounding and unprecedented rate.

Recently, official Communist groups, along with the SEIU (one of the largest workers' unions) and other labor groups, marched in downtown Los Angeles. They were demanding workers' rights (a la Communism), and their signs and banners proudly displayed communist mottos and graphics, along with pictures of Lenin and Che Guevara. Many of these groups want immigration "reform," which ultimately means allowing undocumented workers to come to and remain in the United States while receiving government handouts at the expense of the taxpayer. Many will work under the table here, taking U.S. dollars back to their own land without paying taxes back into the U.S. system.

The obligatory signs and banners that mocked the Tea Party were also in view during the march. The Tea Party is routinely made to appear as a demonic source that if left unchecked, will be the downfall of this country. Of course, it's not explained how this group that wants separation of church and state, less governmental intrusion, and fiscal responsibility within government will accomplish this, but the facts don't matter to unions and those who see Communism and Socialism as the answer to this country's problems.

Within politics, we see a severe disconnect between those in Washington and those outside. The few individuals who are willing to speak the truth and stand up to the system are quickly targeted and relegated to the back of the bus, treated as though they are single-handedly attempting to bring this country down.

Beyond this, we have wars and rumors of wars continuing to expand throughout many regions of the world. In spite of cease-fires that are allegedly in place between Israel and neighboring countries, the bombs that are lobbed into Israel have never ceased. The majority of people throughout the world view the state of Israel as the *problem*. Get Israel out of the Middle East and peace would be the result, or so they think.

In other areas of the world, ethnic and religious cleansing is occurring as never before in recent history. Christians are either being forced out of their home countries or slaughtered for staying. Persecution of Christians is at an all-time high, often ending in death.

So it doesn't matter that what we are seeing is a tremendous push by demonic forces using politics, nature, geo-political boundaries, and social agendas to accomplish their goals. All that matters is that what we are facing is like some great tsunami that we can simply look at, aghast, and wonder if the end of the world has come. It is on its way.

After the earthquake-created tsunami of Northern Japan a while ago, there were many video clips of the event posted on the Internet. As the water broke over the protective walls, it careened down streets, swallowing up anything and everything in its path. Cars, trees, ships, homes, and certainly people became part of the wall of water that would not be stopped.

In some of the videos people could be seen and heard wailing with fright. Some are heard to say things like, "*the end of the world has come,*" because that is exactly what it felt like to them. The only way to find a safe place from the oncoming deluge was to go to higher ground, and in some cases, that didn't even make any difference. The vicious force of the water needed to play itself out before receding back into the ocean. Total and unparalleled destruction was the result.

This is something like what is happening now, with one exception. The demonic waves of spiritual activity will *not* recede. They will grow in stature and in force until nothing stands in their way. God is allowing it, and these demonic powers will not run themselves out, eventually receding back to the hellish cesspool from which they eventually came. They will continue to build to a crescendo until they are stopped by the arrival of the only Person who can do anything about it: *Jesus*.

When Jesus steps foot back onto this planet, His presence will mock the roar of demonic forces and in one word will silence them. Jesus is the only One who can accomplish it, but in the meantime, authentic Christians have a job to do, and that is what we need to be focused on.

Chapter 5

Ministries: Big Business

There is obviously something happening in America and throughout the world that has actually been going on for quite some time. Unfortunately, and as usual, most within the visible Church seem completely oblivious to it.

People often look to leaders of ministries – whether they are church or para-church organizations – to give them the Word of God. They want to be spoon-fed and told what they should believe. They want to trust in what they are hearing. They look up to the people in the pulpits and heads of large ministries and trust that what they hear those people say is the truth, so help them God.

But there is a problem with this – a huge problem. Too many within Christendom do not think for themselves, and in fact, they do not *want* to think for themselves. They only open their Bibles on Sundays or when they attend some conference on the Bible or the End Times. When they return home, they toss the Bible back on the shelf, waiting until the following Sunday or for that approaching convention before taking it down again.

Too many within Christendom prefer to feel *good* about themselves in spite of what is happening throughout the world, including America. It has become too burdensome to read the Bible to gain insight and wisdom or to put on the full armor of God (Ephesians 6). It's far easier to trust in the viewpoints of others as they tell it. We want to go through life laughing and feeling good and so we naturally seek out those who will provide us with what we seek. We see this phenomenon not only occurring within churches, but within para-church ministries. People look up to the pastors and leaders as if they are the final arbiters of truth and realism.

Added to this problem, we see that there are any numbers of ministries today that have grown to become super-sized. By that I mean they have become businesses – *big* business. They began small, depending upon the Lord to show them the way. After a while, they began to "gain respect" within the visible Church. They then grew into something far larger than what they had started out being, and now there seems to be no turning back. In fact, to them the very thought of it means a falling away because success within Christendom – like in the world – is often measured in *size* of ministry, not in actual numbers of people who turn to the Lord for salvation. We forget that there were many times that people actually turned away from Jesus. If we judged His ministry on the basis of the way we judge ministries today, we would say He was indeed a complete failure at times. Yet, spiritually speaking, we know this is the furthest thing from the truth.

In other words, at least some of these ministries have ceased to be ministries *per se* and have become huge non-profit *businesses*. Outwardly they still try to think and act as though they are merely ministries, yet in many cases, it is clear that their motivation is no longer relegated to the realm of ministering to people and certainly not to ministering to the Lord or bringing glory to His Name. They are far more concerned with the bottom line. What *sells*? How can they make a larger return on their investment, whether the investment is in their books, videos, music, or speaking engagements?

The decisions many of these ministries make are based solely on dollars and sense, though they would very likely deny that. The questions asked are questions like, what will bring in the best return for our investment? That is not a question a Christian asks. It is a question a corporation asks. The excuses are given that they must have a return on their investment in order to further the kingdom of God, as if God needs money in order to save people.

However, just a quick look at the type of men Jesus called to be among His apostles tells us that He had a far higher concern than marketing Himself. Had He been concerned about getting the most for His investment, He likely would have gone with some of the Pharisees. After all, they were already well-known among people and either hated or highly respected for the position they held in the community.

Jesus was not concerned about adding any of those men to His ranks as apostles. If they came to Him with the desire to follow Him, that was one thing, but He was not about to add any Pharisee or other religious leader to His small band of men that changed the world. Can you imagine what would have happened had He done so? Of course,

He did not, nor would He ever, add any of them simply because of what they believed and what they stood for, as well as their view of their own self-importance they carried.

Paul is exceedingly clear that the time just prior to the beginnings of what is called The Tribulation in Scripture, the world will see and experience a *great falling* away. This apostasy is inevitable. It *will* happen and it is *now* happening. It references a time in which people will no longer care about the truth and will prefer lies instead. We've mentioned this. These lies tickle their ears. *"For the time will come when they will not endure sound doctrine; but wanting to have their ears tickled, they will accumulate for themselves teachers in accordance to their own desires"* (2 Timothy 4:3). This is the major factor in precipitating this falling away from the truth.

This is how Paul describes it:

> *"Do not let anyone deceive you in any way, for it shall not come unless the rebellion takes place first and the man of sin, who is destined for destruction, is revealed."* (2 Thessalonians 2:3)

The word "rebellion" here is translated from the Greek word that literally means to adopt a mind of apostasy, or to fall away from the truth. This is tragic and too often it doesn't happen overnight, but over *time*. That it happens at all is the tragic part.

But why does it happen? Apart from the aforementioned quest for dollars, there are other reasons, but they all eventually point back to the dollar simply because they are derivatives of it. Once ministries grow in size, they often begin hiring people. The more they grow, the more people they need to have on-board because of the variety of responsibilities that have become part of running such a large organization.

This not only applies to ministries, but also to publishers of Christian books. Too often, books are published by Christian book publishers based not on content, but on *name recognition*. Think of some of the well-known authors that are alive today. It goes without saying that the next book they write will automatically become published simply because of *who* they are, not necessarily what they stand for within Christian circles. Too many books today that are on the best seller's list are nothing more than spiritual pabulum. They appeal to people because they tickle people's ears and nothing more. The end result is that the person reading the book *feels* good, but since they are not learning the truth of Scripture, that's all that happens, and that is unfortunately very fleeting. People who live to have their ears tickled must constantly be looking for other sources that will continue tickling.

The Bible doesn't tickle. It causes growth: true growth. Sometimes the path to growth is painful, but it is always worth it. This is what is meant by Jesus in John 15. There He speaks of the need for the authentic Christian to bear fruit. But bearing fruit will also require *pruning*, and pruning is never fun, though it is always necessary.

Consider bookstores that sell Christian-related materials. The same observations apply to them that apply to some of these megaministries mentioned above. Why? It is because these bookstores are a business, first and foremost. Go into most Christian-type bookstores and you will see books of all sorts (though of late, it seems fewer and fewer are critical commentaries and far more fluff), but you will often see far more than just books.

Whether it's "New Testa-MINTS" or other schlocky candy and items for sale, the truth is that with many businesses that claim to be somehow connected to Christianity, the bottom line is that profits need to be made. In some sense, we understand this when we are talking about *businesses* that begin as such and remain that way (though there is still something very odd about selling candy with Scripture verses on them). I also find it fascinating when I go to bookstores that sell books by well-known authors who tend to disagree with one another. In matters of orthodoxy and important doctrine, both authors cannot be correct, yet that store will stock the books because each author has his or her own set of followers and the store knows that those books will often fly off the shelves.

It's a bit more difficult to appreciate a ministry that seems to grow so large that it has little recourse but to move toward ecumenism or some other aptly known "ism" that simply means the ministry has now gone off the path toward apostasy. There is nothing wrong with getting along with people. There is something *drastically* wrong with compromising solid beliefs in exchange for something that ends up being apostasy, all in the name of "getting along."

We are seeing this at alarming rates: churches who wind up embracing something questionable at best because it seems to be the most expedient thing to do to remain "alive" and "growing." Jesus would have none of that and neither did Paul. When Peter got caught up in error in the book of Acts, Paul stepped right in to lovingly confront Peter and to let him know in no uncertain terms that his compromising was simply wrong (cf. Galatians 2:11). Paul didn't mince words with Peter, trying to save his feelings. He did what was necessary to keep truth afloat. Paul was used by God to prune Peter so that he would bear more fruit.

Ask yourself this question: if Jesus were physically present with us in this world today, how do you believe He would react to many of these ministries/businesses that exist in His Name? Would He appear on the TBN network, for instance? Would He hobnob with people who had questionable stances doctrinally? Would He fear the Roman Catholic Church, or Islam, or other large religious organizations, and would He keep from telling the truth because of it?

Would Jesus purchase and own a Christian bookstore? Would He do His best to build His ministry so that it got so large that it resembled a Fortune 500 company? Would He have multiple mansions?

Look, do we really need to ask these questions? The truth of the matter is that judging by how Jesus lived while He physically traveled this earth it is obvious that He *never* marketed Himself. The Holy Spirit did that. Jesus never went out of His way to find donors for His ministry. He never hired anyone or made them officers on His ministry's board of directors.

This is part of the big problem today with ministries. Living in the United States, and under the tax laws of the same, I started a non-profit ministry and did so under the established and legal guidelines of the IRS. This is the law of the land, and while I realize that some of my brothers and sisters in Christ reject this idea, that's up to them and it is between them and the Lord. They have their reasons and for them, those reasons are good. I'm concerned only with myself and my life before God.

I went with a non-profit because it seemed like the right thing to do in a land governed by the tax code; it allows people to donate to Study-Grow-Know Ministries if they feel so led to do just that. They receive a legal notification from me each year that their donations were received, and because of that they have a right to a tax deduction.

One of the questions that I had to answer while filling out all the paperwork for the IRS was whether or not anyone in Study-Grow-Know Ministries would be on the payroll. The answer is a resounding *NO*. I have no plans to pay myself or anyone associated with my board or this ministry, and I clearly stated that on the application. Any and all money that is taken in through donations is used for the direct purchase of radio time and publishing our books. That's it. No one gets paid. There is no 401k set up for either me or my wife or anyone else connected to the ministry. There is no expense account to dip into. My wife and I work outside this ministry, which provides us with an income to live.

Some might ask, why do I need a board of directors? Isn't the fact that God is overseeing the ministry good enough by itself? In some ways, yes, of course it is; however, there is nothing wrong with having a group of other Christians (hand-picked by me) to be on the board so that I can go to them for advice if necessary. It forces me to be accountable – humanly accountable.

In the United States, all religious non-profits must have a board of directors, but to see some of the people that are on many of the boards of these giant ministries, the question becomes, why was that person chosen to be on a board for a ministry that supposedly represents Jesus Christ? It's a very good question and one that prompts sincere soul-searching, or at least should, for the ministry in question.

I know some religious (even *Christian*) non-profits that have politicians on their boards. This is not to say that all politicians are bad or evil; however, it is almost mandatory within political circles to learn to compromise with others in order to get laws passed. Others have individuals who have clearly strayed away from the true gospel of Jesus Christ and have embraced a form of ecumenism. One can only be left to wonder why, in some cases, there is a need to have such "big name" celebrities on a board if not for contacts and marketing purposes, as if God is completely unable to provide for that ministry if it is, in fact, His ministry in the first place?

There are too many ministries today that have become extremely large and have little choice anymore but to stay the course, even if that means getting into bed with the latest ecumenical flavor of the month. They have bills to pay, salaries to provide for, and the idea of not being able to hop a plane to attend the latest religious convention is not something they wish to deal with, so they continue to play it safe. They would prefer to offend as few as possible and try to please as many people as they can because it is important to keep those donations coming in. I don't see that in Scripture, do you? It did not seem to be something Jesus concerned Himself with, though I'm sure He spent much time in quiet, private prayer about it.

What many seem unaware of is Paul's reference to that falling away that will occur (and already is occurring), as previously mentioned. It is a surety and something that can neither be denied nor ignored. It's happening and it is unfortunate to see some of the "big names" within Christendom leading the way toward rebellion, though it shouldn't surprise. The stage is being set for the Antichrist to make his appearance. There's certainly some time yet, because according to the timeline set forth in the Bible detailing the birth pangs that must occur prior to the beginning of the Tribulation, we still need to see six of them before the Tribulation kicks off. Only three have occurred according to Scripture.

Regarding those birth pangs, we need to see the Northern Invasion spoken of by the prophet Ezekiel (Ezekiel 38-39). This attempted invasion will be led by Gog of Magog, and together with a number of other nations that surround Israel from all directions, their attempted invasion of Israel will begin. When these armies reach the Mountains of Israel, God will step in and take care of the problem. Why? He will do it for the sake of His Name. Ezekiel makes it *clear* that God defends Israel *not* because of Israel, but because of His own precious and holy Name.

After this attempted invasion occurs and is soundly routed, we will need to see the next birth pang: a one-world government. That's coming too. How do I know? Because in Daniel 7:23-24 the Bible says that this will occur. This final Gentile kingdom will engulf the *entire* world. Daniel is not simply seeing or referencing the "known" world, but he is being told about the coming government that will affect the entire world. The world will become *one*.

There are people who are completely unable to see what is happening in the United States and throughout the world, even though it is right under their noses. Either that or they are fully misunderstanding the signs and warnings. We are quickly moving toward a coalesced one-world government. It will happen because God's Word says it will happen! People can deny it all they want, but the truth is there for anyone who cares to notice.

Once we get to the one-world government stage, we see the emergence of the "ten toes" spoken of in Daniel 2 (see also Daniel 7:24a). It makes sense that the one-world kingdom would be broken down into ten manageable sections *after* becoming one, with one individual overseeing each portion.

By the way, if you think this is far-fetched, the infamous group the Club of Rome took the entire world and broke it up into ten sections some years ago (on paper). Go ahead and do a search on it and you'll very likely find a copy of the same document that I found. Question: why would any "club" need to spend their time breaking the world up into ten parts? Plans for the future maybe?

Once we get to this ten section stage, it is then that we will see the Antichrist begin his ascent to his throne. This will be the perfect time because he will now see exactly who stands in his way and it will just be a matter of getting rid of a few of the leaders (three to be exact) in order to secure the allegiance of the remaining seven.

The Antichrist's rise to power is foretold in Daniel 7:24b and 2 Thessalonians 2:1-3. He is at first the eleventh little horn, and after getting rid of three other rulers, he becomes the eighth (see also Revelation 13).

Because of the darkness of the current days and times, it is very likely that the individual the Bible refers to as the Antichrist is alive at this very moment. His identity is of no consequence right now and will not be known until he rises to the top of the heap after the one-world government is divided into ten manageable portions. Then his secret identity will be revealed to the world, just as Paul notes in 2 Thessalonians 2. Of course, the world will not recognize him as the Antichrist. On the contrary, they will see him as savior of humanity instead. He will not only sweet-talk his way into the hearts of millions of people the world over, but he will sweet-talk his way into the hearts of the leaders of the Jewish state, and that represents the ninth and final birth pang: the signing of the 7-year covenant with Israel and her surrounding enemies. He will somehow be able to bring to fruition what no one before him was ever able to accomplish. There will be "peace" on paper with Israel and in the Middle East, and it will actually appear as if the world can now move forward having dealt with this very serious issue. This is the event that kicks off the Tribulation because it will be at that point that Israel will have literally sold her soul to the devil and God will have reached the end of his patience.

We are living in dangerous times, very likely what the Bible calls the End Times. Paul said this to Timothy in his second letter to his protégé:

> *"But realize this, that in the last days difficult times will come. For men will be lovers of self, lovers of money, boastful, arrogant, revilers, disobedient to parents, ungrateful, unholy, unloving, irreconcilable, malicious gossips, without self-control, brutal, haters of good, treacherous, reckless, conceited, lovers of pleasure rather than lovers of God, holding to a form of godliness, although they have denied its power; Avoid such men as these. For among them are those who enter into households and captivate weak women weighed down with sins, led on by various impulses, always learning and never able to come to the knowledge of the truth."* (2 Timothy 3:1-7)

This is a description of what people will become and are now becoming. Friends, we are seeing this today, and it is not simply affecting or infecting non-Christians, but it seems clear enough that it is becoming just as integrated into the visible Church, as previously noted.

There are simply too many churches and ministries that appear to have come off their original moorings. At this point, I'm not interested in naming names. I would prefer people do their own research, and believe me, the research is out there, making it easy to find for the person who truly wishes to find it.

Too many are giving way to the enemy of our souls these days. We are focusing on the wrong thing instead of realizing that our war is *not* against flesh and blood (people) but against powers and principalities in heavenly places (demons and devils). Many are falling prey to this type of thinking and it is doing irreparable harm.

In 2 Peter 3:3-7, Peter warns his readers of this:

> *"Know this first of all, that in the last days mockers will come with their mocking, following after their own lusts, and saying, 'Where is the promise of His coming? For ever since the fathers fell asleep, all continues just as it was from the beginning of creation.' For when they maintain this, it escapes their notice that by the word of God the heavens existed long ago and the earth was formed out of water and by water, through which the world at that time was destroyed, being flooded with water. But by His word the present heavens and earth are being reserved for fire, kept for the Day of Judgment and destruction of ungodly men."*

This sentiment – the question as to where God is and why is He taking so long to return if He actually exists – is not merely being stated by those in the world. It is happening in the visible Church. I know people (and you probably do as well) that mock the idea of the physical return of Jesus, yet they call themselves Christians.

It almost seems as though the bigger a ministry or church gets, the more difficult it is for them to stay the course! It seems they have to spend more of their time trying to figure out how to remain large so that they will not lose what they have gained. In doing so, they eventually start watering down the Word and end up becoming complicit with people who are anti-Bible from the start.

I hear all the time from people who tell me how difficult it is for them to find a church that preaches the Bible. Many have resorted to joining other believers in homes for Bible study, fellowship, and encouragement.

Too many churches do not care. Too many ministries are looking to the bottom line. How is it possible to serve God while constantly considering the profit margin? It isn't.

I believe that God is calling His people – His true Church – to come out from among them and be prepared for a time when things get far worse than they are presently. I'm *not* saying to turn your back on your local church! If you are in a church where the Bible is believed and taught, the Lord has truly blessed you. You need to pray constantly for your church's leadership so that they will not fall into temptation to begin looking at bottom line instead of God's Word to light the way. Stay put! Invite others.

There is a good deal that is happening today, and Christians must be alert to it. Admittedly, it is easy to become sidetracked through involvement in politics or other concerns like safety in society, considering the hateful and inciting rhetoric that is being spewed from any number of sources these days. It is too easy to focus on the individuals who are spewing as opposed to recognizing the power that is *behind* those people. I could name names and provide examples, but the crux of the problem lies not with those people but with the Dark Lord and his minions who constantly work to tear this world and its citizens down. These beings stand adamantly opposed to God and

His authentic children. That is the real problem, not the people who wind up doing Satan's bidding. Yes, they are culpable, but their work is often empowered by the enemy himself. Remove the enemy's power and their work amounts to nothing.

Too many within the visible Church are concerned about their 401(k)s, feeling good about their life, and simply wanting to enjoy what they have without worrying. We have to move on from that. We have to get beyond it because if we do not, it will be our undoing, our downfall.

Be willing to stand against error wherever you find it with all love and gentleness. Be willing to stop buying someone's books or materials simply because they are well-known if they are getting off the authentic path and leading you away from truth and down the path toward apostasy.

In many countries throughout Europe and Africa, Christians are being persecuted as never before in recent history. They are being jailed, abused, and even killed because of the hope they have in Jesus Christ. Evil people are being used to accomplish this, but the ultimate source is the same that it has always been: *Satan*.

I recently read a news story on the 'Net in which three Christian men were murdered in Turkey. Two were converts *from* Islam to Christianity and one was a Christian missionary from Germany. Five Muslim men pretending they wanted to know more about Christianity befriended these Christian men. One day, they went to their offices, tied them to chairs, and simply slaughtered them by slitting their throats. The Muslims had been pretending all along until such a time as was convenient for them to murder the three Christians. We could get angry at the Muslim men, which is our natural inclination, but the truth of the matter is that this evil is what they've been taught to believe is truth! They are lost and need our prayers.

I'm not relaying this story to get people up in arms. In fact, the wives of the Christian men came out and publicly forgave the Muslim men for what they did. Their young children, while they miss their fathers, know that they now live with Jesus. They know that their fathers were martyred for the cause of Jesus Christ. The actions of the martyred men and their families speak loudly, far more than words can accomplish. Who knows, but maybe the extended forgiveness by the families will eventually be the precipitating factor that brings at least some of these Muslim men to the Lord.

The powers that exist behind these terrible acts of murder will continue to push people to do what they want them to do. One day, the Power – the Holy Spirit – that restrains these diabolical spirit beings (demons) will move aside, and when that happens, hell's demons will pour out onto the earth, wreaking havoc on the denizens of this planet.

Folks, this is starting to happen on a large scale. We are seeing it from all sides. Do *you* see it? Are *you* concerned for the lost? In a day and age when too many ministries have become too large for their own good, we need to get back to basics and once again focus more and more on introducing the lost to Jesus. It is as simple as that. Don't become part of the problem. Be part of the solution, and the only solution that truly saves is Jesus.

Chapter 6
Looking Beyond the Obvious

It is way too easy to narrow our focus as we go through life, and we often do this out of a sense of self-protection. After all, if we took the time to take in what was happening throughout the world on a daily basis, we might, in all likelihood, wind up becoming depressed and entirely self-focused, because much of it is not pretty. Evil is difficult to face.

However, I am suggesting that we *widen* our focus, not narrow it, in order to arrive at a better understanding of what this world is coming to and what God is doing *in* the world. We've already discussed a number of things that pertain to how the enemy of our souls is escalating his attack on mankind and the world at large in order to bring his own purposes to realization. He's doing it in ways that appear in some cases to be somewhat innocuous, though when we truly understand what is going on, we have to admit that it is anything but that. Satan is fighting for his very survival, and because of that he will not willingly allow anything to stand in the way of achieving his goals.

So what have we learned so far about how Satan works? We've learned that there are portals in the universe through which spiritual entities – both fallen *and* unfallen – travel either to accomplish God's purposes or to attempt to thwart those purposes. It seems clear enough that these beings – both malevolent and good – reside just on the other side of the dimensional barrier that God set up after humanity fell in the Garden of Eden (Genesis 2-3). Because we do not see them or the dimension that they exist within, it is very easy to become too focused on the things that happen in this world as if *people* are creating the problems directly. This is not to say that people are free of accountability. It simply means that though they have wittingly or unwittingly partnered with demonic entities, the source *behind* the person is the final responsible party.

If we go back to the Garden of Eden, we note that both Eve and Adam were guilty before God and were declared as such. Yet God also promised judgment against Satan as well (Genesis 3). He did not escape (and neither did the serpent he used to tempt Eve), and anyone who aligns himself with Satan and his will to overthrow God will also be judged in the same way.

We've also learned that there is so much happening in the world today that it is very difficult to grab hold of all of it and really absorb it. We cannot keep up with everything that is transpiring throughout the globe. It is impossible, and more than that, we are not privy to the inner workings of Satan's global elite, who willingly do his bidding.

I've written other books that go into detail regarding how Satan is methodically using rock music, New Age mantras, and everything in between to gain as many followers as possible. The most annoying thing is that while he works to achieve such a massive following of people, he himself remains unabashedly in the *shadows*. Such will not always be the case though. One day, a man will walk out onto the world's stage and will be the devil incarnate. He will have all of Satan's power and intelligence.

Think of what this world is building toward. We've talked about the fact that we are moving toward a one-world government, and after that happens, we will then see the world divided into ten sections, each controlled by a "king," as highlighted in Daniel 7. At that time, the Antichrist will begin to scale the wall in order to reign supreme.

What we need to understand is that *everything* in life is moving in that specific direction. It doesn't matter what subject we are dealing with, either. Liberalism has become so liberal that anything that even smacks of being conservative is under severe attack. The reason for this is because in order for the plans of Satan to progress so that the Antichrist can ultimately take center stage, people need to get to a point of believing that we will, one day, all get along, but this can only occur if people stop thinking in terms of individual rights. Individuals in society must give up personal and individual rights (especially religious rights) in exchange for the *whole*. That is becoming the growing mantra for the future. It's not so much individuals that make the world what it is; all of us together...*as one*...will do more than we could by ourselves. This viewpoint needs to be adopted for the "good of all," just as it was adopted in Genesis 11 with respect to the Tower of Babel under the leadership of Nimrod. There, because the people had literally become one in mind, scope, and purpose, God indicated that there would be nothing that humankind would not be able to accomplish. This is exactly the goal that world leaders have once again.

The conservative viewpoint still places value on the individual person and individual rights, something that liberalism cannot put up with, and if left in place, conservatism would forestall any chances for liberalism to become the overarching law of the entire world. It is imperative that conservatism be eradicated in order for humanity to embrace the coming world's destiny: the new world order.

So it does not matter if we are talking about Islam, rock music, New Age ideas, the Charismatic movement and their astral projection to the third heaven, or anything else that exists. All of these areas are playing a role in bringing this world to the next cosmic plane, which is to unify everyone into believing and living the old adage "all for one and one for all." Gone will be individual mandates. This is why capitalism will have to be set aside (except for the very rich, of course, which will retain their wealth). We see history repeating itself, but few seem to notice what is going on or care because they are too afraid of the current, perceived, and coming upheaval.

The powers that be want the world to be in complete dread because it breeds confusion, and when confusion reigns, people tend to yearn for peace above all things. If you look at the political scene today, it is easy to see how this works.

I tend to believe that many situations that occur in this world are earmarked for obscurity by the media, while other situations are used to create a sense of hopelessness and even abject fear. Certain incidents are used solely to incite. Though it seems almost accidental at times, it is clear that these situations and events are used for a greater purpose, the greater purpose of becoming one throughout society. Remember, Satan quite often *prompts* people's reactions.

I believe this is the case with the Trayvon Martin situation. In it, George Zimmerman shot Martin to death in what Zimmerman claims was self-defense. Under current Florida "Stand Your Ground" law, because Zimmerman said he was being physically assaulted by Martin, he had a right to self-defense, even if it meant *lethal* use of it in order to escape with his own life.

Because Martin was black and Zimmerman *looks* white, the media unloaded both barrels on the situation, doing their best to create a racially-charged environment when in actuality it likely has nothing to do with race at all. Once the race-baiting machine went into overtime, it held sway over the media and people. The damage was being done. People like Al Sharpton and others quickly grabbed up the headlines and continued to move the situation toward solid racially-charged grounds.

It was quickly pointed out that Zimmerman, who has one parent who is Caucasian, is a "white-Hispanic," a label that had never been used before, to my knowledge. The point was that the media was attempting to portray this as a *racial* incident, and how better to do that than by pitting a white person against a black? It wouldn't go over as well had Zimmerman been thoroughly Hispanic, so the "white-Hispanic" label was adopted by the press for good measure. It was unnecessary, but it most certainly served its purpose.

Of course, it was not long before we saw the entrance of radical racist Al Sharpton and things really began heating up. Sharpton is probably best known for his stance with respect to the Tawana Brawley and Duke Lacrosse team cases, in which in each case he deliberately sided with the black individuals in spite of any of the facts that tended to exonerate those who were being accused (Tawana Brawley's accusations against a number of white New York police officers turned out to be complete fabrications, and the black woman hired as a stripper to entertain the Lacrosse team members who charged that she was raped also turned out to be a liar). He still says he is right in spite of civil lawsuits that show his guilt.

In the Trayvon Martin situation, once Sharpton got involved there, the race-baiting rhetoric ramped up severely, assisted by the inclusion of the New Black Panthers who summarily put out a bounty of first ten thousand and then one million dollars on George Zimmerman's head, *dead or alive*. During this time, the Department of Justice remained publicly silent, and the only thing that Mr. Obama said was that if he had a son, he might have looked like Trayvon Martin. This remark and the silence of the DOJ served to continue the racially charged rhetoric. Rather than attempting to calm the situation, the powers that be did what they could to ramp it up, even if it meant remaining silent. It became clear that the current administration wanted to see where this situation would take itself and offered nothing by way of oversight and leadership.

The absurdity of the situation quickly grew out of control with black celebrities tweeting what was believed to be the address of George Zimmerman's parents (it was thought Zimmerman was in hiding there since originally the police found no evidence to arrest him because of the previously mentioned "Stand Your Ground" self-defense law in Florida).

This entire scenario created quite a scene with hundreds of people gathering outside the house protesting and generally making life miserable for the occupants. To make matters worse, it was learned that the people who lived there were in no way related to George Zimmerman, but this initially did not stop people from continuing the protest.

Just as the situation grew to its climax, a new prosecutor stepped in to say that they were putting out an arrest warrant for George Zimmerman for second degree murder. Zimmerman turned himself in and is awaiting trial, out on bail.

Interestingly enough, Alan Dershowitz weighed in on the circumstances and stated that Angela Corey (the lead prosecutor) could be in a legally dangerous position because of the 2nd Degree Murder affidavit she produced. *"'This affidavit,"* he said, *"submitted by the prosecutor in the Florida case is a crime. It's a crime. If she in fact knew about ABC News' pictures of the bloody head of Zimmerman and failed to include that in the affidavit, this affidavit is not the truth, the whole truth and nothing but the truth."*[9]

Dershowitz went on to say:

> *"Now, one of the problems,"* he continued, *"is because they've indicted for second degree murder — and there's nothing in this affidavit that suggests second degree murder, the elements of second degree murder aren't here — the expectations have been reduced. There's an article today in one of the... the Daily Beast saying "there'll be riots in the street if there's an acquittal." If there are riots, it's the prosecutor's fault. Because she over-charged, raised expectations. No reasonable jury is going to convict based on the evidence I know of second degree murder. So this prosecutor not only may have suborned perjury, she may be responsible if there are going to be riots here for raising expectations to unreasonable levels."*

In this case, prosecutor Angela Corey was *voted* into office. She was essentially appointed to "get Zimmerman," according to Dershowitz. Yet she had the audacity to stand at a press conference and deny that they indict due to public pressure. That unfortunately seems to be *exactly* what has occurred.

Gone are the days of an unbiased media (if there really ever was such a thing). Because of the way the media played its cards in this situation, Zimmerman will likely *not* get a fair trial. However, whatever

---

[9] http://www.theblaze.com/stories/liberal-legal-scholar-alan-dershowitz-calls-prosecutors-affidavit-in-zimmerman-case-a-crime/ (accessed 04/27/2012)

the verdict, there is a strong likelihood that someone is not going to be happy and will demand blood. During the time prior to Zimmerman's arrest, it came to light that at least one producer at MSNBC doctored the 911 recordings, editing them to make it appear as though Zimmerman used a racial slur when in fact, when the recording is played in its entirety, no such slur exists. Since then, another producer has been fired for altering something else.

Beyond this, a separate media outlet appeared to doctor photos of Zimmerman in custody shortly after the deadly assault took place so that no visible cut or scratch could be seen on the back of Zimmerman's head. Mr. Zimmerman had originally argued that Trayvon Martin had punched him and knocked him down, jumped on top of him and banged his head into the ground. In the photos/video shortly thereafter, no bruising or cuts appeared. It was only after the video/photos were enhanced for actual clarity that bruises could be seen. Moreover, even more recently, photos have come to light which show a good deal of blood seeping out of the back of Mr. Zimmerman's head (photos referred to by Dershowitz).

One individual, commenting on not only the Trayvon Martin situation, but on at least one other situation in which a gang of blacks attacked one lone white individual, offered insight into the situation:

> "In covering the Trayvon Martin case, the mainstream media has reverted to the bad old days of the Jim Crow South '...where complexion counted more than facts in determining how people are treated.' The only difference between then and now is which complexion receives favored treatment by the media.
>
> "The mainstream media has purposefully distorted its coverage of the Trayvon Martin killing by editing its words and graphics to fit its slanted point of view. For example, the mainstream media continues to show the same photographs of Trayvon as a cute 12 – 14 year old little boy, but has yet to show one of the 17

year-old young man who was strong enough to overpower George Zimmerman's [sic] and slam his head repeatedly into the pavement.

"The mainstream media continually refers to George Zimmerman as a 'white Hispanic' because one of his parents was white, but they have never referred to President Obama as a 'white African' because his mother was white. The only conclusion one can draw from this fact is the mainstream media uses the term 'white' only when it suits its nefarious race-baiting purposes to do so.

"The word games the mainstream media plays '...grow out of a notion that complexion tells you who is to be blamed and who is not.' Guilt and innocence should be determined by the facts in a given case, not skin color.

"Perhaps the media is suffering from 'White Guilt' over the abominable treatment of black Americans during the Jim Crow days of Bull Connor and crowd. Thomas Sowell had this to say on that issue: 'Let us talk sense, like adults. Nothing that is done to George Zimmerman—justly or unjustly—will unlynch a single black man who was tortured and killed in the Jim Crow South for a crime he didn't commit'."[10]

All of this is to say that we can sit here and blame the media for what happened, and certainly they are in the wrong (and admitted to it, with MSNBC firing the producer of the segment in which the 911 recording was edited), but by doing that, we forget who is behind the entire charade. It is *Satan*.

People are certainly used by Satan and they bear that responsibility, but the buck stops with him completely. All the evil in the world can

---

[10] http://patriotupdate.com/articles/now-thats-justice-for-trayvon-media-complicity-in-mob-violence#.T5h96ssA68w.facebook (accessed 04/25/2012)

be traced back to him, and the humans involved in specific acts were merely puppets utilized for the moment or for that series of events. Truly, in some cases, Satan chooses to use specific human beings for extended periods of time to help him achieve his short and long-term goals. We see this with many godless dictators that have been used by Satan to create a nation the way he wants that nation created. Hitler, Stalin, Idi Amin, Pol Pot, and a host of others come to mind – individuals specifically used to further Satan's nefarious agenda, while in most cases, that specific dictator may have had no real clue as to the fact that he was being used by the worst malevolent force this universe has ever known.

Satan controls most things in this world. It is *his* world. His power is far greater than anything human beings can understand or wield. His intelligence far surpasses that of the most intelligent among us. Satan is the one who pulls the strings and we too often forget that because we only see the human side of things. Reminding ourselves of these facts can help us to be more effective in preaching the gospel.

In the example of the Trayvon Martin situation, the media wants us to see one thing and that one thing is *racism*. Racism plays well in the media, and when you have race-handlers such as Al Sharpton in the mix, a good show is guaranteed. George Zimmerman was recently released from jail on $150,000 bond and Twitter went wild with death threats as well as threats of race riots should he be found innocent of second degree murder. Race riots could well be in the cards for the global elite. Surely Satan benefits greatly from it, should they occur.

But again, behind the media, Sharpton, the New Black Panthers and all the other black supremacists, one thing stands, but stands deeply shrouded by the shadows: Satan himself.

We need to look beyond the obvious to understand what lurks in the darkness. We need to recognize that behind Islam, behind the corruption and cronyism of politics and politicians, behind the severe doctrinal problems with too many religious groups to list here, and behind racism, one lone figure stands, defiantly posed with his fingers in each of these areas and many others. It is *Satan*. He is the source of sin in this world, and humans, while complicit, still have opportunity to be freed from his tyranny through the gospel of Jesus Christ.

Everything that takes place in this world occurs because it must reach its predetermined end. There must be a one-world government and that government must break into ten manageable pieces. Once there, the Antichrist can rise to power, and he will be the Absolute Imperialist, with only himself to answer to and everything in the world to control.

All of this must come to pass. It will come to pass and it will do so because God *says* it will.

Chapter 7
Not Against Flesh and Blood

As noted, the plain fact of the matter is that according to the Bible, things do *not* go from bad to good, to better, and to best. They go from bad to worse, then absolutely terrible, *then* good. The "good" only happens because Jesus returns to this earth and destroys Antichrist and his minions.

I have written about what Jesus refers to as the "birth pangs" in other books (*End of the Ages* and *Living in the Last Generation*) and touched on them briefly in this one. In those books, I detailed these birth pangs with charts and numerous Scripture references. The birth pangs that Jesus speaks of in His Olivet Discourse (Matthew 24, Mark 13, and Luke 21) are evidences of how bad things will get *prior* to the start of the Tribulation period. Once the Tribulation period begins, life on planet earth will become unbearable for most. This is not an indication that good things are going to happen. It is clear that very bad things will occur before Jesus returns to begin to set things right.

Without going into great detail, note that the birth pangs leading up to the start of the Tribulation are the following:

1. *Nation rising against nation, kingdom against kingdom.* This is a Jewish idiom meaning total conflict in the area in view. In this case, Jesus is referring to a global conflict, something that affects the entire world at the same time. This occurred with WWI. (Matthew 24:1-8; Luke 21:20-24; Isaiah 19:1-4)
2. *Israel a nation.* This occurred in 1948 when Israel once again regained her independence. (Ezekiel 34:11-31; Isaiah 11:11-12:6)
3. *Jerusalem United.* This actually occurred at the end of the Six-Day War of 1967. While this war was not predicted in Scripture, the result of it was, with all of Jerusalem becoming united under Israel's sovereignty. This is the way things are today on paper, in spite of the fact that the Arabs have been allowed to continue to control the Temple Mount. (Daniel 9:27; Matthew 24:15; see also 2 Thessalonians 2:3-4)
4. *Northern Invasion of Israel.* This is yet future and is disclosed to us in Ezekiel 38:1-39:16.
5. *One-world Government.* This is clearly highlighted in Daniel 7:23-24. The world will become one, just as Satan attempted to do in Genesis 11 with the event of the Tower of Babel. He will be allowed to succeed this time.
6. *Ten Kingdom Stage.* Once the world coalesces into a one-world government, breaking it down into ten manageable

parts will be the next stage, and this stage will continue into the Tribulation period. (Daniel 7:24a)
7. *Rise of the Antichrist.* The individual Paul refers to as the "man of sin" will make his move once the world is broken into ten sections. Why now? He will be able to see who he needs to overcome in order to rise to the top of the heap. (Daniel 7:24b)
8. *False Peace and Security.* There will be a time of false peace and security. People will believe that things are finally coming together, but of course this will not hold up. It merely gives the Antichrist time to move things forward while everyone thinks that things are fine. (1 Thessalonians 5:1-3)
9. *Seven-year Covenant.* This is foretold to us in Daniel 9:27 and this is the signature event that begins the Tribulation. Once Israel enters into this agreement for peace with neighboring Arab nations, the people of Israel will have signed an agreement that effectively sells their souls to the devil. God's patience comes to an end and the seven-sealed book of Revelation 5 is opened.

There is nothing in the above list, with the possible exception of the 8th birth pang (*False Peace and Security*), that indicates anything other than the fact that life on planet earth moves from bad to worse. We can see how things are ramping up as they move toward the beginnings of what the Bible describes as the Tribulation/Great Tribulation.

Even before Israel became a nation in 1948, the world was never at peace. With the events of WWI and WWII, we know that the world had done everything it could to eradicate Jews. Hitler killed over six million of them, and while most everyone realizes this, according to the Bible we seem destined to repeat it, this time with Antichrist leading the charge.

With the rise of Islam, anti-Semitism has grown exponentially throughout the world. Movements against Israel have developed to a crescendo of late with a good deal of hate-speech being spoken. Many more even deny that the Holocaust actually occurred but prefer to believe instead that it was merely a carefully crafted lie promulgated by Israel to gain the world's pity.

The truth of the matter is that things are getting *worse*. Whether it's politics, wars and rumors of war, nations rising against nations, the weather, social unrest, ethnic cleansing, or what have you, things in many portions of the world are becoming unbearable and there appears to be no relief.

Those who say that the world is getting better are fooling themselves. Evil will reign *until* the end.

2 Timothy 3:13 states this very clearly: *"But evil men and impostors will proceed from bad to worse, deceiving and being deceived."* If this is what existed in Paul's day and he was able to realize that this would mark global society as time marched onward toward the end, how much more corrupt, deceived, and deceitful have men and women become in today's society, roughly 2,000 years removed from Paul?

Moreover, if, as Paul states in Ephesians 6:12, our battle is not against flesh and blood, but against spiritual entities in the heavenly realms, why are so many within Christendom acting as if our war *is* against flesh and blood? Why do we take the time to stand against other people and corporations who do what they do *because* of the fallen spiritual entities *behind* these flesh and blood faces?

If Paul tells us clearly that we are not in a battle against *people*, but in fact, we are in a spiritual battle against *fallen angels* in order to *rescue* people *from* the kingdom of darkness, then why do we tend to see other people as our enemies? Because they are physically right in front of us and it is them that we see.

There seems to be a fine line between wanting justice in the world and fighting against "evil" corporations and people to achieve that purpose. If you are aware of a need in someone's life, you are obligated to at least attempt to meet that need if you are able. This is the meaning of the parable of the Good Samaritan (cf. Luke 10:25-37; see also 1 John 3:17-18).

In that parable, we note that a man was attacked, robbed, beaten, and left for dead on his way from Jerusalem to Jericho. First, a priest came along, saw the man and deliberately passed by on the other side of the road. He offered no help at all.

Second, a Levite came along and, upon seeing the beaten man lying on the side of the road, also chose to pass him on the other side, leaving a wide berth. Finally, a looked-down upon Samaritan happened along this same road, but instead of ignoring the man, he made a deliberate attempt to help him.

The Samaritan took the man to the nearest inn. There, he asked the innkeeper to take care of the man and nurse him back to health. The Samaritan paid the innkeeper, promising that on his way back through he would square accounts with him if the money he provided was not enough to cover the expenses for the injured man.

This is a perfect example of what God expects us to do as we travel through this life. As we see a need, we are to do our best to meet that need. I must confess I have not always done that. Ultimately, every person has the exact same need: *they need salvation*. Sometimes, we need to alleviate physical needs before a person is ready and able to hear about their spiritual needs.

However, many within the church today go much further and believe that protesting our government – either local, state, or federal – in attempting to change situations for people is the right thing to do. Frankly, I do not see where peaceful protesting comes into play for the Christian when we are dealing with corporations and people who do things that we believe are unjust. I do not see an example of organized protesting in the Scriptures.

Once we begin to protest, we are actually pitting ourselves against other *human beings*. I'm wondering, if instead of using our time to organize protests and boycotts, which wind up placing us squarely against other people, we took the time to *pray* about these situations, entering into spiritual battle there, what such spiritual activity might bring about? Would it bring about change in *individuals*? Would it open doors for us to present the gospel?

Again though, what are we hoping to *change*? Do we believe that if we can create a society that appears to be in line with our definition of Christianity then we will be able to lean back on our haunches, believing that we have accomplished some measure of good in society? What about the people we are effectively standing against through our protest? Have they learned anything about Jesus and the salvation He offers? Have our efforts created a thirst within them to know the truth and embrace Jesus, or do they simply see us as pitting our understanding of right against what is believed to be their erroneous version of right?

I realize that this is a bit of a slippery slope because people's beliefs and attitudes toward this world run the gamut and are often emotionally charged. Many believe that United States, for instance, was founded upon Christian beliefs, and because of that we only need to *repent* and this country (America) will "be saved" because God will once again extend His mercy to us. The problem is that the United States is *not* Israel. God is not taking His covenantal Remnant from the United States to form the final Israel. With the exception of national Israel, God does *not* save countries. He saves *people* and He does so one by one.

Paul also tells us in another portion of Scripture that our *citizenship* is not on this earth, but *in heaven*. Here are Paul's words to the Philippian believers:

> *"Brethren, join in following my example, and observe those who walk according to the pattern you have in us. For many walk, of whom I often told you, and now tell you even weeping, that they are enemies of the cross of Christ, whose end is destruction, whose god is their appetite, and whose glory is in their shame, who set their minds on earthly things. For* **our citizenship is in heaven**, *from which also we eagerly wait for a Savior, the Lord Jesus Christ; who will transform the body of our humble state into conformity with the body of His glory, by the exertion of the power that He has even to subject all things to Himself."* (Philippians 3:17-21; emphasis added)

We need to allow that reality to sink into our hearts. Here, Paul compares and contrasts those who do *not* know Jesus with those who *do*. He calls people who are not saved "enemies of the cross of Christ" and he makes that point with *tears* because his heart goes out to them. He wants them saved. He also notes that our true citizenship is not even *on* this earth, because it is in *heaven*.

He describes these unsaved people not only as being enemies of the cross, but as those who will eventually be *destroyed*. These individuals are dead set against God and His mercy and grace. They are so focused on the things of this life that they are unable to see that there is life beyond this life. They live to continually feed their own wants and desires. They have no concerns about what happens after they die. It's all about the here and now, getting as much as they can for their lives now. They are completely deluded and deceived.

For the Christian, the ever present truth is that we are not citizens of this planet because our citizenship has literally been *transferred* from this present kingdom of darkness to the Kingdom of Light, God's

Kingdom. That should create a strong desire within to want to see others trade up to that same citizenship through Jesus Christ and His gospel. Our citizenship creates an ownership within us and prompts us to do things for our particular country.

There is nothing wrong with appreciating the many freedoms that Americans enjoy from being citizens of America (or your own country). However, even here, those freedoms should be used to reach others who do not know Jesus. At the same time, we cannot depend upon the consistency of those freedoms and must always be prepared to tell someone else about Jesus, even if it one day becomes *illegal* to do so.

Consider just one country in North Africa and what it is like to be a Christian there now. If you live in Egypt right now – in the middle of 2012 – and you are a Christian, you are likely undergoing severe persecution. The chances of losing your home and watching your church building being bulldozed right in front of you are great. The possibility of even losing your life because of your faith in Jesus is very high. Why? Because Egypt is undergoing ethnic cleansing due to Islam leading the charge against those who are not of Islam. Muslims there believe that Allah would have them purge Egypt of all religions because to them, only Islam is the way and the truth. All others are false and an affront to Allah.

We cannot blame Muslims for how they think. In fact, they believe that what they do, they do to gain the blessings of Allah. As a Christian, I know these individuals are wrong, and it would be easy to want to fight against what they are attempting to do in this world with their belief that a new caliphate (Islamic rule) is coming over all the earth. Yet, that pits me against another person, when the real problem lies in the *spiritual* realm.

Behind these zealous Muslims stand powers and principalities that care nothing for Christians *or* Muslims. They hate all people because people were created in God's image, and Satan and his minions hate that reality, since they were not. Prior to Satan's fall, he as Lucifer was God's highest created being, but in spite of that he was not created in God's image.

After Satan's fall, he crafted a plan to bring down humanity in order to bring dishonor to and eventually overcome God. That has been his plan from the beginning and it is that agenda he continues to push and will push until the end. He has made great gains throughout the entire world, yet he has only been allowed to do what God has given him permission to do. He is busy infecting the entire world.

Egyptian Muslims, because of their belief in Allah, have decided that what is necessary is eradicating, by any means, all other religions. I firmly believe that Allah is simply Satan dressed up in another form of religious garb in order to seduce and deceive the masses.

Satan uses Muslims to persecute and kill Christians in Egypt and elsewhere. It is because these Muslims believe that their citizenship lies within Allah's kingdom that they believe they have a responsibility to cleanse this earth from all religions that are not Islamic.

All Muslims *need* Jesus. They are currently empowered by the god of this world (2 Corinthians 4:4) because they reject the one, true God. Their god is using them to destroy Christians. While these Muslims are certainly liable for their actions, they lack understanding because they erroneously see their religion as the truth. They are blind to the truth. Their need for Jesus is not even something that registers on the radar. In order for them to see that need, Christians who are being persecuted – some even to death – must be the light of God in that corner of the world. They must willingly place themselves in God's care for a far higher purpose than simply having freedoms in Egypt to worship as they choose to worship.

The greatest need for Muslims, as well as all unbelievers, is that they come to know that Jesus is the way, the truth, and the life (cf. John 14:6). How will they come to know that if people are not willing to lay down their life in full submission to the glory of God? Christians who love God and prove it by obeying Him wind up *abiding* in Him (John 15).

As noted, because we might be citizens of a particular country on this planet, we tend to feel a strong connection to it. That connection often pits us against others who seem to want nothing more than to bring a country or world to its knees. I believe this connection we feel to our country often colors the way we act in the world.

Tell me, have you ever felt that you are an American *first*, a Christian second, and something else third? You may not recognize it, and you may also believe that you are a Christian first. I would encourage you to take this entire subject to the Lord in prayer asking Him for His discernment so that you can understand if you are actually placing your country of birth above Him.

But consider if you became an ex-patriot of your current country and chose to adopt a new country as your home. Because you were not born and raised in that particular country, you likely would not have the same burden for it. Because of that lack of burden, it would be easy *not* to take things so personally when laws or regimes change.

We have *ownership* in the country we were born in, and therefore when things happen in the country of our birth that we do not like or agree with, we feel a sense of duty to right those wrongs.

But in truth, when we became Christians, we became citizens of another *country*, if you will. That country – *heaven* – will never have a regime change. It will never put up with injustices of any kind, nor will lawlessness hold sway over it.

It is very difficult for us as Christians to fully come to grips with the fact that 1) our citizenship has been transferred *from* the kingdom of darkness to a place called heaven, and 2) our job as Christians is to fight for the very souls of people who *remain* in the kingdom of darkness. Sometimes we are way too earthbound for these truths to sink in and become real within us.

When Jesus walked this earth, the Jewish leaders were expecting a "messiah" to come along who would free them from the tyranny of Roman control. They did not find this in Jesus. Had he come as a conquering hero, dressed in armor, carrying a sword, with fire flowing from His mouth and a physical army behind Him, they would have no doubt accepted Him as leader, but even then, not necessarily as Redeemer, Savior and Lord.

The Jewish leaders wanted someone who was going to fight their battle for them, not someone who came along to teach about loving your enemies and doing good things to those who despitefully use you. This was a message they were not at all interested in hearing. This was a large part of the reason Jesus was rejected.

What the leaders and many others failed to see was that Jesus Himself stated that He was not part of this world (cf. John 15). He readily acknowledged that Satan was the ruler of this world and because of that, Satan had no part in Jesus at all. John 15:18-19 says, *"If the world hates you, you know that it has hated Me before it hated you. If you were of the world, the world would love its own; but because you are not of the world, but I chose you out of the world, because of this the world hates you."*

Considering Jesus' life, do we see any instances of Jesus standing up to or against the government of Rome? Do we see Him organizing and leading protests at all? No. What we see instead was a God-Man who *lived* the life of an obedient servant, submitting Himself to the rule of Rome as long as doing so did not circumvent His Father's will.

In essence, Jesus placed Himself under the feet of the Roman authorities because He knew that those in authority were placed there by God.

In the life of Paul, do we see examples of him trying to buck the system? Do we see him portrayed as a ringleader trying to amass the troops to overthrow Roman rule? No. Instead we see a man who, like Christ, lived to tell others about the gospel. That was Paul's main driving force. He wanted others to know the truth of the gospel so that they might come to know the One who grants eternal life.

Paul's entire adult life after becoming born again as recorded for us in Acts 9 was to work to bring others out of the kingdom of darkness into God's Kingdom of Light. In Acts 25 – 26, we see Paul's witness before kings and rulers. He longed to tell people about the saving grace of his Lord Jesus Christ so that they would also gain eternal life! He could have had his freedom except that he had appealed to Caesar, and he did that because he knew it would take him straight to the rulers of Rome where he would be able to explain the gospel message to them.

Paul did not work to overthrow the government by outwardly attempting to intimidate its leaders or by creating an undercurrent of unrest among the populace. What would have been the point of that?

We have too many people who call themselves Christians today who are doing that very thing. They try to rally the troops, creating a situation in which Christians protest and attempt to create change in society, when no such example that I can find exists in the Scriptures.

We are wrestling against powers and principalities in heavenly realms. We are *not* wrestling against people, though Satan may work to create that illusion so that we come to believe it.

I have seen – and you have too, I'm sure – protests by Christians which come to a head against others who stand against Christians and Christianity. What is the result? Is anyone saved because of those gatherings and protests? It is very difficult to know.

Some take it so far that they believe they can murder in God's Name because of the crime that someone else is committing. For instance, a number of doctors who worked in abortion mills have been gunned down by people who *call* themselves Christian. These misguided murderers fully believe that they are doing what God wants them to do because of the murders committed by the abortion doctor. Obviously, they have completely missed our Lord's message. Where in the Bible does it allow for Christians to go out and kill other people?

Of course, I believe that abortion is fully wrong. It is unconscionable that unborn babies are aborted at the rate of 1.25 million plus annually in America alone. This is nothing short of wholesale murder, and certainly, God is greatly grieved. Yet He purposefully stays His own hand because we are living in the age of *grace*. If God is not going to slay those who commit abortions, how does it become our job to do that, especially given the fact that abortions are *legal* in the United States? God *will* deal with it in His time.

It is one thing to stand outside an abortion clinic and pass out tracts or attempt to talk to the often misguided women who use abortion as birth control. It is quite another thing to take the law into your own hands by taking the life of another human being. The former is legal (unless of course the abortion clinic obtains a restraining order), while the latter is fully illegal, not only by society's standards, but also by God's standards.

Our job as Christians is to be a light to this world and to pull people from the flames. This is what Jude tells us. *"And have mercy on some, who are doubting; save others,* **snatching them out of the fire***; and on some have mercy with fear, hating even the garment polluted by the flesh"* (Jude 1:22-23; emphasis added).

Paul spent at least three years in Ephesus. He worked hard there, first bringing the gospel to the Jews, and after they wholeheartedly rejected the message, Paul went to the Gentiles. From there, Paul worked tirelessly, battling with prayer in the spiritual realm, and he saw the results of his toil. Many became Christians in Ephesus.

Interestingly enough, Ephesus was the center for a great deal of pagan worship. It was at one point the trade center for the ancient world. There were a number of temples and edifices built to various gods. Ephesus was the home of the *Artemesium*, a monolithic temple built for the worship of Artemis and one of the seven wonders of the ancient world. Artemis was considered to be the goddess of fertility.

Within the temple and as part of the process of worship, temple prostitutes plied their trade with those who came to worship. Many immoral things were done in the name of worship at Ephesus, as well as in other cities throughout Asia Minor.

It is fascinating that, though I'm sure these pagan practices grieved Paul's heart as the Lord's, he did not start a movement to *protest* their wickedness. He did not try to shut down the various temples in order to make society a better place for those who lived there. He did not pray against these pagan beliefs, as far as we know. He continued to simply and powerfully spread the gospel.

Paul did not become politically involved to outlaw the practices of temple prostitution that existed as part and parcel of worshiping Artemis (as well as other deities in other cities Paul visited). He did not storm city councils attempting to change accepted societal norms.

Paul attacked the problem *spiritually* and in so doing, helped many find their way out of that pagan and pantheistic lifestyle and into a living relationship with Jesus, the Author of life and provider of salvation. The *secondary* results of this caused an interesting problem that we learn about in Acts 19.

Because of the fact that people became authentic believers, they no longer needed or wanted to buy the artifacts that were used in the worship of Artemis. This created a problem for silversmiths like Demetrius because it affected their wallets. If more people continued to become Christians, they would no longer need these artifacts. If they no longer needed the artifacts, then Demetrius would lose his source of income.

So Demetrius did the only thing he knew how to do. He organized a protest against Paul because of the fact that his business was negatively impacted by those who converted to Christianity, and ultimately, Demetrius saw Paul as the problem. I find that interesting, don't you? Paul simply goes about his business to evangelize the lost. Because of his work among the heathen, the Lord begins opening the eyes of the blind so that they will see the truth found only within the gospel of Jesus. Once their eyes were open to the truth, many of them embraced Jesus as Savior and Lord. Because of the change within them produced by the new birth, they realize they no longer needed the silver shrines of the goddess Artemis so they stop buying them.

Not only was Demetrius affected, but so were the other businessmen of Ephesus who also made shrines and other artifacts for worship. Demetrius succeeded in getting these other businessmen all worked up so that something might be done to halt Paul's efforts among the populace. Without realizing it, Demetrius was being used by Satan to stop Paul. Do you see that Demetrius was simply a pawn in the hands of the powers and principalities that Paul speaks about in Ephesians 6? Demetrius was not the problem. Satan was and remains the problem. Demetrius was used as a tool by Satan to overcome Paul's efforts and to cancel out the effects of the gospel. Yes, Demetrius was fully responsible for what he did, and he has been judged for it. But the real problem is that Satan as the god of this age (and the age that Paul lived in) causes unsuspecting people to do his bidding.

Notice the reasoning that Demetrius uses to create coalescence with the other businessmen of the area: *"Not only is there danger that this trade of ours fall into disrepute, but also that the temple of the great goddess Artemis be regarded as worthless and that she whom all of Asia and the world worship will even be dethroned from her magnificence"* (Acts 19:27).

Note that Demetrius not only brings up the fact that Paul's efforts are hurting their business ventures, but – to throw a bit of religiosity into the equation – he also points out that the temple of Artemis itself will be seen as something worthless and Artemis herself will be tossed aside.

If people would only stop to hear what they are saying to realize how empty their words can be. Demetrius admitted that Paul's efforts wound up *hurting* the image of Artemis, yet the false goddess Artemis was obviously not powerful enough to do anything about it, so the businessmen of the town were the ones required to do something. I find that very interesting, don't you? That's the way it is with paganism. People worship gods who cannot do anything to help themselves.

The argument certainly implies that Artemis is not so great because one human being – Paul – is in danger of bringing her and her temple down into disrepute. Why do people worship things like this that are made with human hands? It is because they are blind. They are blind because they do not have the gospel of Jesus. They do not have the gospel of Jesus because too many Christians are concerned about changing society instead of changing lives by introducing people to the Person of Jesus.

Unfortunately, instead of worshippers of Artemis, it could have been Muslims, because this is exactly what they believe: that they have to do things *for* Allah because Allah seems incapable of doing anything to save himself or make the world a better place unless his adherents fight his battles for him. This is why terrorists exist. It is also why people who strap bombs onto themselves do what they do. It is because Allah can't. This tells me that Satan is allowed to exercise only so much power, and if he doesn't have people fighting his battles for him, he would not be able to accomplish as much as he has even accomplished today. Satan wants authentic Christians to become sidetracked into fighting against *people* instead of introducing them to Jesus.

Back in Ephesus, even though a near riot breaks out over this issue, Paul wants the opportunity to talk to the businessmen. Paul's friends would not allow it because they believed that he would have been torn limb from limb, or at the very least tossed into jail and left to rot.

Who was it that organized a protest? Demetrius, worshipper of Artemis (Satan) did that. Why? It was due to the *results* of Paul's evangelistic efforts. It hit Demetrius where it counted, and apart from that, he likely would not have cared about what Paul was doing or saying. Ultimately, though, Satan was losing followers to Jesus and he didn't like that at all. He watched as people were transferred from his kingdom of darkness to God's Kingdom of Light.

Notice that Paul never went on a frontal assault against the temple of Artemis, those who worshipped her, or the silver smiths. Paul essentially took the gospel to the lost people of Ephesus and because of it many became authentic believers in Jesus and a number of churches were started. Because of *that*, these new believers stopped purchasing silver shrines connected to Artemis. That was a direct hit to the wallets of the businessmen in the community and it was at that point that they began to push back against Paul. Christian, Satan will hit you when he begins to see that your evangelistic efforts are pulling people out of his kingdom into God's Kingdom.

Here in America, people have the freedom to protest peacefully. We have the right to work within the system to create and change laws. Because of these rights, things for good can be accomplished. However, the greatest change is not done when a good law goes into effect. The greatest change is accomplished when a lost soul becomes born again, or authentically saved (cf. John 3). Their citizenship changes from the kingdom of darkness to God's Kingdom. Their life changes and they begin to no longer need or want the things that they used to need or want. This *will* affect Satan's business.

I'm wondering if too many Christians today aren't putting the cart before the horse. Many believe that if we can change the tone of society, then *people* will change. Has the law prohibiting murder *stopped* murder? Have all the anti-drug laws worked to create a drug-free society? Just the opposite is true. People need to be changed from *within* and then society will change. Yet even with that, this world is still heading toward a collision course with God's judgment. We cannot escape it. The most we can do is escape eternal *judgment,* and that only occurs when we become authentically saved.

The truth of the matter seems to be that it doesn't even matter how many people in society become authentic believers, society will *still* not change for the better. That will only occur when Jesus steps foot back onto this planet, enters into judgment and then rules with a rod of iron. That is what will change society. No amount of self-effort on the part of people will accomplish what only God will do.

We all want society changed for the better. Many believe that they can do this through the political process. If God has called you into politics in order to affect change in society, then He has obviously done so for a purpose. Changing laws can go a long way toward righting some of the wrongs within our society. However, unless you are actually called into the arena of politics, I suggest you don't go there, because it will be too easy to get caught up in the problems associated with that political arena, which may sidetrack you.

Politics often wind up pitting people against one another, and because of that people become blind to the fact that people need salvation. As a politician – even a Christian politician – your overriding reason for being a politician may be to overturn Roe v. Wade, a seemingly good aspiration. If that's what you believe God would have you do, then you have an obligation to do that. You will probably not be successful in getting it overturned because Satan is too well ensconced there for that to happen. Yet the Lord may use you on a personal level to be a witness to other politicians around you so that they begin to see the light of Christ in your life and want to know why you believe the way you believe. It may open doors for you to witness to people who otherwise have become thoroughly jaded about God. Seeing your Christianity in action may be just what they need to open their eyes to the truth of the gospel.

I believe that this is the way we need to be thinking. We should not be entertaining the thought that we are going to change the physical world or the mores that define society because I do not believe that this is why God keeps us here *after* we become authentic believers. He keeps us here on this planet so that we can spread the gospel of Jesus, warning others of their impending doom and offering them the good news of Jesus Christ. The most we can do is offer the truth to people. Whether they embrace that truth or *not* is not up to us, but God. It is our job nonetheless to consistently share the gospel of Jesus Christ, whether people listen or not.

Is your overarching concern in life making society a better place to live or is it seeing people come to know the Lord? If the former, then I suggest that you do some soul searching, prayer, and Scripture reading. If the latter, then I believe you understand what the will of the Lord is above all things.

Chapter 8
As It Was in the Days of Lot...

Looking to the saga of Sodom and Gomorrah, we see something that *should* penetrate our souls. Lot lived in a day and age when blatant homosexuality and all manner of sexual perversions existed. The people of Sodom and Gomorrah did not even try to hide it, according to the Bible.

I know...I know. Many gay activists have offered all types of explanations for why the twin cities of the plain were destroyed. Of course, all of their explanations conveniently avoid any discussion of gay sex, whether man on man, man on boy, or something else entirely.

It is not my goal here to castigate homosexuals. I simply want to bring out the facts as noted in God's Word. People are free to disagree with me and likely will.

A number of things existed during Lot's time in Sodom and Gomorrah, and we glean from the Scriptures that even though Lot lived among these people, he was not a homosexual himself. We first learn of Lot in Genesis 13. He and his uncle Abraham had a problem getting along, so Abraham asked Lot to choose for himself where he would live and Abraham would go the other way. Lot did so and the two separated.

In Genesis 14, we learn that a number of kings decided to come against the kings of Sodom and Gomorrah and wound up taking Lot captive. Abraham learned of this and went after him, ultimately freeing him from being imprisoned. This is also the chapter where Abraham meets King Melchizadek and ends up giving him a tithe, but that's another story.

Segue to Genesis 18 and we learn of a visit of three men to Abraham. Abraham asks them to stop and eat, and during the course of the conversation he learns that Sodom and Gomorrah are marked for destruction. Abraham goes through his famous *"Will You indeed sweep away the righteous with the wicked?"* (Genesis 18:23) and asks the Lord if He would destroy the cities if 50 righteous people were found there. He continues until he reaches the number ten, and the Lord assures Abraham that he would not destroy the two cities if ten righteous individuals lived there. Unfortunately, it becomes clear that fewer than ten lived there.

In Genesis 19, we get right into the thick of it. The two angels who had visited with Abraham are now in Sodom. They are there *not* to save the city, but to save Lot and his family. The text tells us about their arrival: "*Now the two angels came to Sodom in the evening as Lot was sitting in the gate of Sodom*" (Genesis 19:1). Please note that Lot was among those who sat at the gate. Sitting at the gate meant that he was part of the *politics* of Sodom. He was likely a type of judge. When people had problems, they brought their problems to the men of the gate and the men judged between parties to determine who was right and what would be done.

Lot was, in some sense at least, a bit of a politician. This comes up later in the story too, brought forth by some of the men of Sodom who obviously did not like what Lot stood for, and they told him so. We'll get to that in a moment.

Please remember that Lot was involved in some form of leadership and that he was among those who judged between right and wrong and likely attempted to do what was right by God's standards. Peter tells us that God "*rescued righteous Lot, oppressed by the sensual conduct of unprincipled men*" (2 Peter 2:7). This is a reference to the angels rescuing Lot from the twin cities of Sodom and Gomorrah, marked for destruction by God because of their sinfulness. Notice that Peter calls Lot "righteous" and that he endured the "sensual conduct of unprincipled men" on a daily basis.

As the story unfolds, we discover that the men of the city wanted the two angels to hang out in the town square with them so that they could "know" them. Of course, gay activists say that this has nothing to do with the sexual proclivities of the townsmen. They just wanted to hang out. If that's true, then it makes no sense that Lot would offer his two *virgin* daughters to the men in order to keep them from "knowing" the two angels (cf. Genesis 19:5-8). What is Lot thinking?

If the men of the town only wanted to chat and get to know the two angels, why on earth would Lot have offered his two virgin daughters to the men of the town to have their way with them? It makes absolutely no sense…unless, of course, the men of the town wanted a great deal more than to simply chat with the two angelic visitors.

After Lot offers his daughters up, one of the men verbally pounces on Lot, condemning Lot's "judgmental attitude." Notice what he says. *"This one came in as an alien, and already he is acting like a judge; now we will treat you worse than them"* (Genesis 19:9). The reality is clear here. These men did not simply want to talk with the two visitors. They wanted to rape them, and Lot was trying to help them realize how terrible their desires were and was attempting – in a very ineffectual way – to get them to see the light of just how evil they had become by offering his virgin daughters.

So we see a number of things at play here. First, the men of the town *were* homosexuals and intended to have their way with the two visiting men. Second, we note that Lot was somewhat involved in the political arena of Sodom, doing what he could to keep things from getting worse, I imagine. Third, Lot understood that the evil that was thoroughly ensconced within his society because of the men of Sodom was thoroughly evil indeed.

In America today and in various parts of the world, gay activists are doing all they can do to force the world to accept their lifestyle as normal, whether we want to do so or not. They are working at it from two fronts. First, they want same-sex marriage to be seen as being as normal as heterosexual marriage. Second, they want to make any dissension to be viewed as a hate-crime. They know that not everyone is going to come on board with them, so to keep people from sounding off about it, they hope to be able to one day use the law to shut people up. These laws currently exist in Canada, and activists point to them as an example of what should exist in the United States.

By attempting to normalize gay sex, same-sex unions, or what have you, they hope to turn things upside down. They are trying to change psychology, theology, and ultimately society so that no one will be able to work to save anyone from the gay lifestyle. They want all the doors tightly shut by forcing people to recognize as truth the lie that homosexuals are born that way, not created by circumstances. If a person is born that way, then there is no way to change them, and to try to change a person who was born a certain way should be seen as a crime.

In California there is now legislation that, if adopted, will make it impossible and even against the law for therapists to try to help homosexuals come out of the gay lifestyle, in spite of the fact that thousands upon thousands of gays and lesbians *have* come out of that lifestyle throughout the world.

Gay activists, being pushed by Satan and his minions, are doing everything they can to change society so that the world will be forced to accept homosexuals as normal, whether anyone agrees with it or not. Being political about it won't help either. There is no scientific evidence to support their contention that homosexuals are born as homosexuals. In fact, in general, it goes against nature *and* Darwin's survival of the fittest (not that I put any faith in evolution).

In California, Prop 8 came under fire for attempting to define marriage as between a man and a woman. On two separate occasions, people went to the polls and voted to support the idea that same-sex unions were unconstitutional. Even though this was all done within the confines of the law, gay activists were not happy and fought with everything they had to overturn what the majority of people in California believed to be right. Gay activist judges sided with the gay agenda and homosexuals won the day. Prop 8 in California was completely overturned.

Recently, North Carolina went through the same thing and made it law that marriage is between one man and one woman. Gay activists learned a great deal from California, and I cannot imagine that they will leave North Carolina alone without a fight. There will be a large fight, and ultimately, it may be that gay activists will win again in North Carolina.

We are all aware of what has been happening with the recent situation surrounding Chick-fil-A and Mr. Cathay's comments regarding the traditional nature of the family. This of course, set off a firestorm of controversy with gays and those on the Left wanting to censure Mr. Cathay's statements *and* his ability to do business in certain towns like Boston, Chicago, San Francisco, and elsewhere.

It really boils down to a freedom of speech issue, but not to the homosexual. Since they classify any opinion that says homosexuality is wrong as *hate speech*, then they want that type of opinion outlawed. This is what the Left wants to do.

Mayor of Chicago Rahm Emanuel had no problem pointing out that Chick-fil-A values are not Chicago values. I guess putting an anti-Semite like Louis Farrakhan (who is also opposes to same-sex unions because he is Muslim) on the Chicago payroll produces no problem though. Apparently, Mr. Emanuel sees no contradiction here at all in castigating Chick-fil-A, while propping up Farrakhan. This type of hypocrisy is alive and well on the left side of the political aisle.

Moreover, those who protest Chick-fil-A because of the owner's particular set of beliefs see no difficulty in driving *to* a Chick-fil-A (or back home) in their car that uses gas. The gas was purchased at a gas station serviced through OPEC. A number of countries associated with OPEC are Islamic where incidents of executions of young gay men have been on the increase, solely because they are gay.

This type of hegemony that the Left would like to use in their attempts to dominate anyone who does not agree with them becomes obvious. The most tragic part is that it seems clear enough that this particular administration – though originally opposed to same-sex unions – now recently came out in support of them. This position change has contributed to possibly more votes, but at what cost? While pandering to the gay community, Mr. Obama may well have ostracized many more people who are now staunchly opposed to him. Such is the case of the Coalition of African-American Pastors, with membership near 4,000. While that might not seem like much (compared to the gay community), what needs to be considered is not simply those 4,000 pastors, but the full number of people that those 4,000 pastors influence.

The problem with homosexuality is not simply that it is *sin* as others things are also sin. The problem is that homosexuality is a *lifestyle* that affects every part of that person's life. It takes what God has created and literally turns it on its head. Is it any wonder that Paul provides us the downward spiral of this type of problem in Romans chapter one? He starts with a type of *idolatry* and ends with people who are finally given over to their own inner lusts that it becomes what they *do* because of whom they have *become*.

So is it *wrong* to be involved in politics? Not necessarily, because as Christians and legal citizens of this country, we have a right to vote and to be involved in the political process in the United States. The only problem I see is that if we are *only* involved politically in attempting to change things, we can easily begin to see gays and gay activists as *opponents* (or people we are in a battle *against*) instead of seeing them as people who need Jesus and His salvation. When that happens, it becomes problematic because as Paul tells us, our battle is *not* against flesh and blood but against powerful spiritual forces in the heavenly realms (Ephesians 6:12). At that point, we have lost sight of the reality of the true battle.

Politics and political aspirations can only accomplish so much. We may feel that if we win, we have won a victory for truth; but in the end, what of the homosexual who desperately needs Jesus? If we believe that we must, through the political process, do what is right and stand up against the things we believe are unscriptural, it can become easy to lose sight of the fact that many who stand on the *other* side of the political fence opposite us need salvation.

Lot was involved in the politics of Sodom. He was a judge who tried to do what was right (I'm guessing by God's standards) and he could only do so much. In the end, both Sodom and Gomorrah were destroyed because of the heinousness of their sin and their crimes against humanity, not to mention the fact that the stench of their sin had reached God's nostrils.

We are seeing a rebirth of the Sodom and Gomorrah attitude today. It has come to us again, and it makes sense that it would because Satan has always been attempting to do anything and everything that stands against God, His purposes, and His glory. Satan hates people so much that he lives to bring us down to his level. He longs to destroy us and when he can't take our lives, he will settle for bringing us down into the worst living abyss imaginable.

Paul highlights this progression in Romans 1. It's not pretty, but it adequately describes people who not only *want* to dismiss God, but who do everything in their power to live as if God does not exist. In Paul's description, we see that God finally gives them over to their own licentiousness so that they eventually destroy themselves.

In public and to one another, gays will tell you that they are happy. They have no qualms about being gay. It's who they are and how they must live and no one should be allowed to tell them they can't. The trouble is that historically, thousands upon thousands of people have *left* the gay lifestyle to live happy, normal lives in Jesus because God opened their eyes to His salvation and He freed them from the gay lifestyle. They came to understand that homosexuality is wrong and like all sin, God will destroy it. Those who continue to be part of that lifestyle will be destroyed with it. This goes for the lifestyle of any sin, whether it's murder, thievery, prostitution, or what have you. Just look at the text below for the descriptions.

> *"For this reason God gave them over to degrading passions; for their women exchanged the natural function for that which is unnatural, and in the same way also the men abandoned the natural function of the woman and burned in their desire toward one another, men with men committing indecent acts and receiving in their own persons the due penalty of their error.*
>
> *"And just as they did not see fit to acknowledge God any longer, God gave them over to a depraved mind, to do those things which are not proper, being filled with all unrighteousness, wickedness, greed, evil; full of envy, murder, strife, deceit, malice; they are gossips, slanderers, haters of God, insolent, arrogant, boastful, inventors of evil, disobedient to parents, without understanding, untrustworthy, unloving, unmerciful; and although they know the ordinance of God, that those who practice such things are worthy of death, they not only do the same, but also give hearty approval to those who practice them."* (Romans 1:26-32)

Reading these words makes it abundantly clear what Paul meant. I don't have to explain it. You can try to push the reality away if you'd prefer, but that won't change the meaning or truth, except for you.

Ultimately, when people decide they do not want to acknowledge God any longer, God will eventually give them over to a completely depraved mind. It is amazing to me how often people become thoroughly involved in sexual perversions of many types all because they do not want to admit or recognize that the God of the Bible *exists*. Once people begin to do this, they will literally eventually exchange the truth of God for a lie, and that lie conforms to whatever personal proclivities they have within them, sexual or otherwise.

For some, it's homosexuality. For others, it's finding sexual fulfillment through astral projection or in some other manner. Whatever it is, the truth is that people will do whatever they have a mind to do. It is like the words we read in Psalm 2:2-3: *"The kings of the earth take their stand and the rulers take counsel together against the Lord and against His Anointed, saying, 'Let us tear their fetters apart and cast away their cords from us'!"*

In the above text, the rulers are the ones who want nothing more than to be free of God's control and rightful rule. In Romans 1, it's the average person, but in the end, the desire is the same, and it can and does affect all people regardless of position or stature in life.

What people do not realize is that *something* will control them and if it isn't God, it's going to be Satan and his minions. That seems to be okay with too many people, though.

Christians *can* work to try to change society for the better, and we may actually make some gains. How long those gains will last is anyone's guess. If you feel so led to try, then try you must.

However, the greatest thing that a Christian can do is to introduce a lost soul to Jesus. Changing society does not bring about *inner* change for people. Societal changes simply force change upon people on the outside. We hope that they will be kept in check because of rules and laws that are in place, but those rules and laws have no real or lasting effect on the hearts and minds of people.

Salvation from Jesus creates true, permanent change and is the only thing that does. I would much rather stand before the Lord knowing that I introduced people to Him who wound up receiving His salvation and who will join me in eternity with Christ, as opposed to standing before Him knowing that my efforts here merely attempted to change society. I know me well enough to know that if I place a great deal of effort into changing society, I will very quickly start to see people as my opponents instead of lost souls who are in dire need of eternal life.

One of the things that will help me the most is something I've already mentioned. I need to realize that my *citizenship* is not here. It has been transferred to the heavenly realm. I need to learn to let go of this life and this world and realize that my job here is one of *reconnaissance* and *salvage*. I need to find out who needs saving and I need to do all that I can to ensure that they understand the message of the gospel. I need to be in constant prayer for the lost souls of this world and I need to be available to Him so that He will speak and live through me for the benefit of those who do not yet know Him.

I can live my life trying to change *things*, or I can live my life trying to bring a change to *people*. Society as a whole will not be saved. In the end, God has promised to destroy this planet and the heavens, replacing them with brand new ones. One day, everything will change.

God leaves His children here after they become Christians so that they can do the work that Jesus started. He began pulling people from the kingdom of darkness while He walked on this earth. He calls and expects us to carry on His mission.

Chapter 9
A World Going Mad

As indicated, it is difficult if not impossible to keep up with everything that is happening in society today. Changes that are occurring are taking place way too rapidly for us to adequately catalog them, much less stop them, even if we had the power to do so. Unless it is your full-time job to seek out everything that is transpiring throughout the globe, good luck keeping up with it.

Besides the things that have already been discussed herein, just a brief sampling of things that are impacting the world (as this book is being written) is the violence in Syria and other parts of the Middle East, North Africa, and Europe.

Ever since what the media termed the "Arab Spring" began, life in the Middle East has gotten very precarious. One regime after another has toppled. Tunisia, Egypt, Sudan, and Libya have all fallen, and now the world looks to Syria to see if they are going to be next.

Our own current administration has seemed to play a part in encouraging the upheaval, violence, and overthrow. Money and troops were provided for the Libyan revolt, and while the American people were told that the U.S. would simply play a support role, it quickly became apparent that this was not the case and that our troops were being used as foot soldiers in another war. This war was simply called a "kinetic military action" so that obtaining Congressional approval could be avoided since Congress must approve a declaration of war. The current administration seems to live to find ways to circumvent Congress whenever possible. Why bother with the Constitution?

With Syria in the news on a daily basis, we see the bloodshed, the violence, and the death that has become the norm for millions of people living under Assad's regime. Recently, videos began appearing on the 'Net that showed people literally being buried alive as punishment for going against Assad. It is difficult to verify their veracity, but the problem is that no one really knows how bad the bloodshed is except those who live in Syria and are fighting for the overthrow of Assad's regime.

If we couple this with all the seeming improprieties found within our own government, the overall stench of corruption becomes too much to deal with, much less withstand. Add to this the growing threat of Islam and we begin to see that certain forces are moving against the very sanity of this world in order to bring in a new world order.

The Tea Party is known by most as a movement that arose to rebuff the government's wastefulness and seeming corruption. The Tea Party wants less government and also wants a government that is fiscally conservative in its spending. Because of this, the movement itself is being vilified by liberals.

Yet there exists another movement called the Occupy Movement, which lives beyond the edge of law in at least some cases. In spite of this, the media continues to hold the Tea Party to account, but not the Occupy Movement.

Occupiers speak out against capitalism. They want a redistribution of wealth so that the have-nots *have*, while the haves, have *less*. This Robin Hood idea is little more than Communism or Socialism.

Recently Ann Curry ranted in a video that the playing field needed to be leveled with respect to who gets what and how things are done in America.[11] The thing that is most telling here is that people like Curry or Michael Moore (who is worth an estimated 50 million dollars), or any number of politicians and celebrities, never seem to want to spread *their own* wealth. Instead they want the government to do it, using taxpayer dollars.

With the exception of one celebrity, I have not read about any individuals opening their own wallets to help make the world a better place for the less fortunate among us. People rely on the government to do that because it's impersonal. It's only *taxes* that are paid out anonymously, so no real worries.

The few celebrities who do dig deep are normally ignored by the media because this same media is too busy trying to push the Socialist agenda. They want it to fall onto the shoulders of the government, and they know that this will only be accomplished by taking more

---

[11] http://www.mrc.org/biasalerts/nbcs-curry-rants-its-fundamentally-unfair-some-have-more-money-others (accessed 04/26/2012)

from the Middle Class to give to the poor. The rich are never going to be touched. They know that. Warren Buffet and George Soros are safe and so are their millions and billions.

But what else do we see happening? Free speech and freedom of religion are coming under attack from all sides, but interestingly enough, it is mainly affecting conservative and Christian groups. Vanderbilt University recently told a Christian group applying for recognition on campus that they could not include the phrase that states that they want only leaders who are committed to Christ in the group. That was offensive to Vanderbilt so they refused to accept the application from the Christian group until the phrase was expunged. Rather than do that, the group chose to go off campus.

Under the guise of "hate-speech," more and more people's rights are being eradicated. I was speaking with one pastor from Canada who stated that because of the laws that exist there designed to protect gays from "hate-speech," a pastor cannot teach that homosexuality is biblically wrong on the radio or TV. If he does, either he or the station will be fined. Truth is becoming off-limits in some quarters.

In another case, at Western Kentucky University, a pro-life student group set up a *Cemetery of the Innocents* display. There were roughly 3,700 small white crosses as part of the display. However, one student not associated with the group chose to attach condoms to the crosses, desecrating the display. Campus police refused to do anything and the professor of the student placing the condoms "*defended [the placement of condoms] as an example of '[c]ritical engagement with ideas'.*"[12]

However, it became clear that the student who placed the condoms on the crosses viewed the display as an intrusion and said as much. The student's use of condoms was argued to be free speech, while the

---

[12] http://blog.speakupmovement.org/university/freedom-of-speech/free-speech-versus-vandalism-at-western-kentucky-university/ (accessed 04/26/2012)

display of crosses created by the group was not viewed as such. There is a terrible double standard when it comes to what the world is willing to put up with from conservatives and authentic Christians, and that double standard is growing markedly.

In another situation, an atheist group – Military Association of Atheists and Free Thinkers – has put pressure on the Air Force to remove Bibles from their on-base housing for guests. The group wrote a letter saying that the Bibles should not be available in the rooms. As one individual pointed out, instead of wanting to display their own material, they demanded that the Bibles simply be removed in spite of the fact that 85% of military individuals state they are Christian.[13]

All of this is par for the course. Most understand that in the last days, not only will mockers exist, but there will be plenty of situations in which groups like the ones just mentioned come out in full force against Christians and Christianity. It is simply the way the world is going. This is what Satan has to do because of his abject hatred for Jesus and for His authentic followers.

Yet we see a rolling out of the red carpet for groups like Islam, which leaves us speechless. Recently, there has been a growing trend among judges in this country to welcome and even make room for Sharia law within the U.S. court system because of the sensibilities of many Muslims. We are told they come from countries that do not understand the type of freedom we enjoy in the United States and because of that we need to help them make the transition from their country of origin to the United States. We can help in their adjustment period by allowing Sharia law into courts in cases of family matters and practice. This is what radical Islam wants.

The question is, how far do we go? The other question is, why should the United States literally set aside its own sovereignty under the U.S.

---

[13] http://www.youtube.com/watch?v=01RKxhTijeQ&feature=youtu.be (accessed 04/26/2012)

Constitution and Bill of Rights to begin making judgments through the eyes of Sharia law or any other international law? This makes little sense to people who understand the value of our founding documents.

Sharia law is a huge step *backwards* in time. It places women and children at risk and puts the man squarely in the role of dictator in the home. Under Sharia law, the husband can beat his wife publicly, and there are any numbers of videos on the Internet that teach Muslim men the "proper" way to do this. It is horrendous and yet many in the West believe that there is nothing inherently wrong with Islam and that the things that people worry about really amount to nothing because they are exceptions to the norm of Islam.

But are they? In a recent situation in Egypt, something has come to the top that is appallingly grotesque, yet it appears to be the truth. We are aware that ever since Mubarak's overthrow the Muslim Brotherhood has gained power throughout Egypt. Our own administration has encouraged the overthrow of Mubarak and helped to create a place for the Muslim Brotherhood within the political field.

Originally, the Muslim Brotherhood indicated that they would not offer a candidate for president, but would remain on the sidelines, allowing true Democracy to take its course. Recently, they changed their minds and decided to provide a candidate.

What has been happening in Egypt since the Brotherhood began its climb to power? Coptic Christians have been on the receiving end of the persecution by factions of Islam because they want Egypt to be an Islamic country *only*. They do not want churches to exist because they want the country to be fully dedicated to Allah. This cannot happen if they allow Christians to remain and so the persecution has begun in earnest.

But as terrible as this persecution is, there is something that is so unbelievably disgusting it is difficult to write about. As this book is being written, the following has not become law yet, but this author sees little hope that common sense will prevail.

According to one source, "*Egyptian husbands will soon be legally allowed to have sex with their dead wives - for up to six hours after their death.*

The controversial new law is part of a raft of measures being introduced by the Islamist-dominated parliament.

It will also see the minimum age of marriage lowered to 14 and the ridding of women's rights of getting education and employment."[14]

This is from an *opinion* piece in an Egyptian newspaper. It is not being considered in any parliament or political group in which laws are made. However, what civilized society *does* this? I look back at what I just wrote and I find it completely unbelievable, yet that may well be what Egypt's parliament will eventually *consider* under the leadership of the Muslim Brotherhood. Will they successfully bring these measures into law? Certainly only time will tell, and it is hoped that human decency along with common sense will prevail. The mere fact that this is something that a society is even talking about in an op-ed is chilling to say the least. Does Romans 1 come to mind? It should.

We must also remember that many believe that agents of the Muslim Brotherhood have infiltrated the U.S. government at the request (appointment) of the Obama Administration. Some of these individuals appear to be very high up in the government and routinely make policy decisions related to our country's safety. Numerous books have been written about this subject and it has become common

---

[14] http://www.dailymail.co.uk/news/article-2135434/Outrage-Egypt-plans-farewell-intercourse-law-husbands-sex-dead-wives-hours-AFTER-death.html#ixzz1tBp6EsoH (accessed 04/26/2012)

knowledge. It appears that our government has been taken over by radicals.

Beyond all of this, we have a current administration that seems to spend more time (and millions of taxpayer dollars) on vacations than in doing any real work. Every time Mr. Obama heads off for vacation, the taxpayers are charged *millions.* Since taking office, Mr. Obama and/or his family have taken sixteen vacations in just over three years. Who takes that many vacations? While that may seem like nitpicking, the reality is that our economy is in dire straits and needs fixing, but instead of fixing it, the plan seems to be to continue to increase the national debt beyond the ability to repair it!

Federal Reserve Chairman Ben Bernanke recently indicated we are facing dramatic fiscal problems. He said that a *"[f]ailure to take new action by the end of year...would have negative effects on the economy that even the Fed couldn't offset."*[15] He actually calls it a "fiscal cliff."

In spite of this, it appears that this current administration seems unconcerned and continues to move forward, adding to the national deficit like some of us drink water. The reason for the concern is clear. *"Among the expiring breaks are Bush-era tax rates on personal income, capital gains, and dividends; a payroll-tax reduction; and some tax relief for businesses. The foundation says tax changes related to President Obama's health-care reform law are also set to kick in, drawing more revenue from taxpayers."*[16]

Added to the financial problems this country faces, we have another area that adds to the debt and has become a millstone around the necks of many students. Student loans have become a burden too few can handle, especially considering the lack of available jobs for which people have been trained.

---

[15] http://www.csmonitor.com/USA/Politics/2012/0426/Fiscal-cliff-threatens-economy-on-Dec.-31-Bernanke-warns-Congress (accessed 04/26/2012)
[16] Ibid

> *"Here's what we do know about student loan debt: it's roughly $1 trillion in size, greater than either auto or credit-card debt and second only to mortgage debt in the U.S.*
>
> *"Borrowers in their 30s today owe $28,500, on average. The debt burden has soared just as — and partly because — the recession hit, so younger graduates carrying the highest balances are hit with the double whammy of a weak job market (that still isn't showing any sign of rapid improvement).*
>
> *"And this all comes as globalization and technological change have upended once-reliable career paths, wiped out many mid-level professional jobs and leave low-paying fields in health, food and beverage services, and retail as among the fastest growing job markets over the next decade."*[17]

Because of the tremendous increase in cost to go to many colleges these days, most students have had to take out massive loans, and since many to most are currently without work, they are unable to pay them back. What's the government to do? Forgive the debt? There is talk of that, but what will that do to the already overburdened economy? Nothing good.

One of the ways our government is considering reducing the deficit is by taxing Americans' retirement funds.

> *"Uncle Sam, in a desperate attempt to fix its $16 trillion-plus deficit, is leering over Americans' retirement nest egg as its new bailout fund.*
>
> *"Capitol Hill politicians are assessing tax changes that could let the Internal Revenue Service lay claim to a portion of the $18 trillion sitting in 401(k) accounts and other tax breaks used by*

---

[17] http://www.cnbc.com/id/47171658 (accessed 04/26/2012)

> middle-class workers, including cutting the mortgage tax deduction.
>
> "A commission looking for ways to close the deficit, and, noting the extent of 401(k) tax breaks, recommends an examination of the system as one way to prevent government bankruptcy.
>
> "Besides 401(k)s, other possibilities include the mortgage-interest deduction on second homes, as well as benefits from employer-provided health insurance, which are untaxed now."[18]

What we are seeing is a government that has literally run amok, spending money it does not have and working with absolutely no budget (which is *illegal*). Once again, taxation on the Middle Class seems to be one of the ways the government is considering filling the debt hole.

We could go on and on with more governmental problems, but the truth is apparent to those who care about truth. This country – this *world* – is racing headlong into the coming cataclysmic fallout from a total global collapse, and I would not be surprised if the United States winds up leading the way.

---

[18]

http://www.nypost.com/p/news/business/plunder_CrD9s6MElVsElJj2IVgHuK#ixzz1tBuCCw00 (accessed 04/26/2012)

Chapter 10
Age of the "Super Christian"

It's not just politics. It's not simply the kinds of the things that are happening in society throughout the world. It includes the things that are happening in the *visible* Church. We need to see it and we need to uncompromisingly address it, not in judgment (God does that), but with *warning*. People – especially those who *say* they are Christians – need to wake up to what they believe and learn whether or not what they believe is truth or fiction.

Aside from everything that is happening today, whether it's in the realm of politics, societal mores, the revolving door of dictators for certain countries, or what have you, probably the most telling thing that is happening today is in the realm of what can only best be called the onset and growth of "super Christians."

It has become a growing fad with growing numbers of alleged Christians scrambling to the top of the heap. Christianity can be big business. Bestselling Christian authors make millions, and their books, along with public appearances and guest speaking stints, add to their burgeoning star stature.

It certainly appears that success within Christendom comes to those who have special gifts. Whether it's the alleged ability to heal, speak in unknown tongues (with flair), or just be really good looking while holding a Bible, super Christians abound and they have quite a following, which simply makes me wonder.

If we take the time to look at Scripture, we see that the idea of a super Christian would have been unheard of in Paul's day. At the same time, if we were to call anyone a super Christian – apart from Jesus Himself – Paul might have fit that bill, but not in the way we think of it today.

However, Paul would be the first to say (and *mean* it) that he was the least within God's Kingdom because of how much he persecuted the true Church prior to his conversion (cf. Philippians 3:3-6) and, in essence, as he found out on the road to Damascus, persecuted Jesus Himself (cf. Acts 9). Paul was not a man that we would recognize as a super Christian of today. He would be viewed as a *failure*.

After his conversion to Christianity, Paul faced unparalleled persecution himself. He was beaten with rods, left to die, bitten by snakes, unintentionally started riots, was shipwrecked on more than one occasion, and was ridiculed at every turn. He was followed from town to town by Judaizers who tried very hard to discredit whatever Paul taught.

Paul was imprisoned for speaking the truth, something that is coming into vogue in this century. He often had to support himself with the art of tent making. He didn't dress in flashy suits, was not taken from town to town in the best-looking limo, and never stayed in the presidential suite at the best hotel in town. Paul's life ended as a martyr and along the way, he lived to glorify His Lord, Jesus.

Today's super Christian knows none of these things. The people I'm referring to live in complete comfort, like kings and queens. They have homes that are true marvels. They have boats, horses, a fleet of cars, chauffeurs, domestic servants, and everything they need to live a life of luxury that most can only dream about.

Today's super Christians care more about how much money the sales of their books and videos bring in than in really seeing a lost soul come to know Jesus as Lord and Savior. They are in every way like the Pharisees of Jesus' day. They have an outward form of godliness, but they deny its power to *save*. Of course, they would disagree with everything I've just written. They would argue that my words are born of jealousy. The truth is that the super Christians of today are far more concerned about life's pleasantries and how much wealth they can amass.

If you look at the books they write, you will see that they plaster their faces or their entire bodies on the front cover. As they look at the viewer, they beam benignly with a smile that seeks to say that you could also share in what they have if you will only believe that it can be yours. Buy their book and they will share that information with you.

The most interesting thing about these super Christians is that they are never wrong. They have the answers, and if you will but look to them, you will gain access to truth too.

But take a close look at some of these super Christians. Note their antics when they walk in front of a TV camera on stage, with their singers behind them and a hall of admirers in front of them. They preen and prance across the stage. They yell and jump up and down, constantly wiping the sweat from their foreheads. Everything about them says *"this is a show."* They are there to entertain, and the better they entertain, the more money they gather in the coffers.

Marjoe Gortner was a child-evangelist turned actor who at a very young age was taught the tricks of the trade by his Pentecostal mother and father, but primarily his mother. He would go on the show circuit and mesmerize hundreds of thousands of people throughout America.

In his documentary called "Marjoe," he spoke of the good ol' days when the money *flowed*. He talked of the show and how to bring in the money by working the crowd. He spoke of how important it was to excite viewers and those in attendance so that they reached deeply into their wallets and purses. This is what it was all about.

Marjoe was the main breadwinner of his family. It is how his family survived and enjoyed a lifestyle that many during that time did not. Marjoe knew he brought in plenty of money, though he says he rarely saw any of it. It was immediately turned over to his parents.

When we watch the antics of many well-known members of the visible Church, we are privy to the workings of the enemy, whether people will agree with that or not. These individuals have grown accustomed to the lifestyle they have built for themselves and they have no intention of letting it go. It all boils down to the show itself and their love of fame and money.

In Luke 9:57-60 we read these words:

> *"As they were going along the road, someone said to Him, 'I will follow You wherever You go.' And Jesus said to him, 'The foxes have holes and the birds of the air have nests, but the Son of Man has nowhere to lay His head.' And He said to another, 'Follow Me.' But he said, 'Lord, permit me first to go and bury my father.' But He said to him, 'Allow the dead to bury their own dead; but as for you, go and proclaim everywhere the kingdom of God.'"*

Notice that Jesus attested to the fact that He had no permanent place to rest His head, nowhere He could call home. Yet today's super Christian not only has *a* beautiful mansion, but normally a number of them, along with his own personal jet to get him from one place to the other. Flying economy just won't do.

It's remarkably easy to be a super Christian today because all you have to do is make promises to people, based (very) loosely on God's Word, which they will come to believe. Tie it in with their tithes and offerings and the deal is wrapped with a bow of guilt. People will begin to believe that the lifestyle of the super Christian is real because they think it is taught in God's Word. Why do people think that? Because the super Christian *tells* them it is, and moreover, he says that same lifestyle could be the average person's if they will but believe too.

You see, today, the average person would not mind fame and fortune. They think it will fulfill all their fantasies and make them a better person. It doesn't matter how many times we read about people who won the lottery and whose lives were ruined because of it. That does not matter one iota because people will always believe that it will be different with them if *they* win the lottery, or if *they* become the next singing sensation or the next discovered talent.

Fame and fortune is what many want today, and Christians are made to feel good about that when they see super Christians who live the opulent life. It can't be wrong if that super Christian over there has a mansion in Hollywood Hills and one in Colorado. It can't be wrong because just listen to what they preach and read what they teach!

This is the problem. No one really listens anymore. No one really pays attention to the message. Super Christians on the TV have dumbed down the gospel so that they can emit snippets here and there with great exuberance and people will gobble it up.

Who understands today? Who truly discerns? Who knows what truth is as it is taught in Scripture? The Bible has become a book that people use as a proof text to further their purposes (if they read it at all). Few read the Bible in its entirety. Fewer still keep things within their original context. People want Christianity the *easy* way, and the easy way means taking only from the Word what is palatable and easy to swallow. This is the job of the super Christian, to make only parts of the Bible *palatable*. The rest? Just toss it out. Ignore it.

Super Christians seem to abound. They are a group of self-absorbed, self-aggrandizing individuals who belong to a special club, and regardless of what they might like the average person to think, they are really not interested in literally sharing the wealth, because there isn't enough to go around. They have what they have not because they are true to God's Word and worship Him in Spirit and in Truth. They have what they have because they live a lie, a lie that too many people tend to believe and, more than that, wish to *emulate*.

Jesus said that in the last days, things would get so bad that if it were possible, even the *elect* would be deceived (cf. Matthew 24:24). That day is *here*. Now, if the deception is so strong that if possible even the elect would be affected, then how strong do you think that delusion would be?

Fortunately, Jesus said "if possible" referencing the elect, meaning that it *won't* be possible to deceive the elect. However, the delusion *will* be strong and the strength of that delusion would deceive everyone *except* the elect. That says a great deal about the impact of the growing delusion.

There are many people today masquerading as Christians. Moreover, many are masquerading as *successful* Christian entrepreneurs who have succeeded because God has allegedly blessed them. Do not be fooled. God does not judge success as the world does. For God, success happens in the *spiritual* realm.

Yes, God may opt to provide great financial resources to some of His authentic children, but know this: He does *not* do that so that those children can spend that money on making their own lives *easier*. He provides resources in order that *He* will be blessed and glorified.

It is almost too easy for most to fall prey to the lies that are touted and lived by the super Christian. They parade themselves across the world's stage with all their pomp and circumstance and they are worshiped. They need to be shunned, but at the same time, prayed for, because what they are doing does not bring God glory. Maybe God will have mercy on them and open their eyes to their own folly so that they will be saved. That should be our prayer. Instead, too many wind up encouraging them in that lifestyle.

I shudder to think of how Jesus would react to the many people within the visible Church today who are seen as the super Christian if He were physically here on this planet so that we could see and interact with Him face to face. The way certain individuals tell it, they would have no problem slapping Jesus on the back and hanging out with Him. It would be "cool."

A very well known "ministry" (using the term very loosely) was recently outed by a major newspaper. The public is now seeing what has existed for years behind the scenes with the opulent wealth and, might I suggest, tremendous waste, all to keep the two main people of the situation happy and the money flowing. What has been largely shielded from public view has become fodder for the tabloids:

> "The prosperity gospel preached by Paul and Janice Crouch, who built a single station into the world's largest Christian television network, has worked out well for them.
>
> "Mr. and Mrs. Crouch have his-and-her mansions one street apart in a gated community here, provided by the network using viewer donations and tax-free earnings. But Mrs. Crouch, 74, rarely sleeps in the $5.6 million house with tennis court and pool. She mostly lives in a large company house near Orlando, Fla., where she runs a side business, the Holy Land Experience theme park. Mr. Crouch, 78, has an adjacent home there too, but rarely visits. Its occupant is often a security guard who doubles as Mrs. Crouch's chauffeur."[19]

Question: why does ANY so-called Christian need to live so high on the hog?

The entire situation came to light because of infighting among family members of this gargantuan television ministry:

> "Now, after an upheaval with Shakespearean echoes, one son in this first family of televangelism has ousted the other to become the heir apparent. A granddaughter, who was in charge of TBN's finances, has gone public with the most detailed allegations of financial improprieties yet, which TBN has denied, saying its practices were audited and legal.

---

[19] http://www.nytimes.com/2012/05/05/us/tbn-fight-offers-glimpse-inside-lavish-tv-ministry.html?_r=2 (accessed 05/05/2012)

> *"The granddaughter, Brittany Koper, and her husband have been fired by the network, which accused them of stealing $1.3 million to buy real estate and cars and make family loans. 'They're just trying to divert attention from their own crimes,' said Colby May, a lawyer representing TBN. Janice and Paul Crouch declined requests for interviews."*[20]

The tragic thing is that many in the world have likely believed that Paul and Jan Crouch were beautiful examples of God's marvelous blessings, bestowed on the lives of those who lived a true Christian life. Too many within Christendom are willing to believe that if you live for God, you will be rewarded materially with blessings from on high. This is certainly what the Crouches taught and Christendom bought it, hook, line, and sinker. The world didn't buy it, believing that so-called ministries such as TBN's are man-made, deriving their "blessings" from the guilt cues and misguided understandings of Scripture that are regularly foisted upon the unwary or unthinking.

Granddaughter Koper recently explained that "*'[m]y job as finance director was to find ways to label extravagant personal spending as ministry expenses,' Ms. Koper said. This is one way, she said, the company avoids probing questions from the I.R.S. She said that the absence of outsiders on TBN's governing board — currently consisting of Paul, Janice and Matthew Crouch — had led to a serious lack of accountability for spending'.*"[21]

God is not mocked, and whether He takes the time to judge a person or group during this lifetime or the next is His business. Even with the likely eventual downfall of this very famous ministry, there will be others that will slip through the cracks. Moreover, the problem of charlatans posing as ministers or evangelists will continue. This

---

[20] Ibid
[21] http://www.nytimes.com/2012/05/05/us/tbn-fight-offers-glimpse-inside-lavish-tv-ministry.html?_r=2 (accessed 05/05/2012)

should be no surprise to us simply because of Jesus' warning to that extent in Matthew 24, along with the numerous warnings from Paul. One notable text already mentioned is 2 Timothy 3:13, which tells us point blank, *"But evil men and impostors will proceed from bad to worse, deceiving and being deceived."*

Whether the Crouches are outright evil people or whether they are simply misguided Christians or complete imposters is for God to decide. These "super" Christians should not be living like this. Jesus did not. Paul did not. Many other believers throughout the New Testament Scriptures did not and most authentic believers throughout history since then have not. As Paul stated, *"For the love of money is a root of all sorts of evil, and some by longing for it have wandered away from the faith and pierced themselves with many griefs"* (1 Timothy 6:10). Money itself is *not* evil. It is the *love* of money that destroys, and it is one of the oldest motivating factors since the Creation. By it, many gain tremendous power over others and are placed in a special category by the rest. They appear to be untouchable, but there is always the payback, and it will eventually arrive as a heavy taskmaster to those who use money to abuse power and privilege.

The super Christian lacks respect or love for God (if they ever had it) because they seem to be too in love with themselves and their own desires. They have a tremendous sense of *self-importance*. They lack wisdom. They lack many things, in spite of all the material "blessings" they have come to know.

In all possibility, though, the most significant thing they may lack is *salvation*. For all their antics, they are little more than proud showmen, picking the pockets of the average person who refuses to think for themselves. As long as there are people who believe they need to be spoon fed, super Christians will exist and will have a following. That is, until Jesus returns.

Chapter 11
It's Always Been Smoke and Mirrors

God has always had a plan of salvation, and in a sense, so has Satan. God's plan involves saving as many people as possible *from* Satan's kingdom into His and ultimately creating new heavens and a new earth, over which God the Son will reign forever. God's plan of salvation has been relatively easy to comprehend, though, unfortunately, impossible to believe for too many people *be-*

cause of its simplicity. Many have left this life without God, without His truth, and tragically, without His salvation.

On the other hand, Satan's plan has been easy to discern (for the informed). It has always been to wrest (and keep) control of this planet from God and its citizens and to declare himself to be god of all. Coupled with this, Satan has also endeavored to enslave as many human beings as possible in order to keep God's salvation from affecting their souls.

Satan has built into his charade of salvation a convoluted mess of winding avenues that seem to lead nowhere, but through it all, the promise of secret knowledge or *gnosis* is always held out to the initiate. Just as there are many passageways, halls, doors, and stairways that end with solid brick walls in the Winchester Mystery House in San Jose, Satan's most enjoyable method of snaring people has been through the promise of providing spiritual insight by following the maze created by occultism.

Satan did that with Eve and Adam, promising them that they would become like God, who knows good from evil (cf. Genesis 3). If they would simply *submit* themselves to his lie, they would gain immeasurable insight and knowledge. This they did, but the cost was tremendous. All Creation groans from the weight of that failure to continue to follow God's plan (cf. Romans 8:19-24) and looks to the day when the curse will be fully and finally lifted.

People are extremely gullible. From Eve and Adam to present day humanity, people have always chased after the promise of learning the mysteries of the universe. Satan has designed it so that people will believe that the God of the Bible is a selfish and jealous God, not wanting to share real information with any part of His Creation. Though Satan is a consummate liar, people believe him when he speaks as if he is telling the truth and nothing but the truth. He tends to sound authoritative, and just like the ideal con artist, people not only accept his word as truth (despite any misgivings) but tend to hang on every word with bated breath – even waiting for more – in spite of any reservations they might have toward him or his message.

We can go way back in biblical history highlighting specific details of the many times Satan has entrapped those of God's Creation through his ability to lie naturally and without hesitation. Like the master magician who promises his audience thrills and more thrills through one sleight of the hand or redirect after another, causing them to believe that he is truly bending the laws of physics, Satan plies his trade of dishonesty with an ever-increasing web of lies and deceit. The more complex it has become, the greater the numbers of people who seem interested.

If we simply go back to the beginnings of this country alone, we can clearly see (because it has been so often repeated and verified) how Satan gained a foothold in the beginnings of America through those who *founded* this country. It is nearly common knowledge that many to most of our Founding Fathers were Deists. Yes, they cited the Bible and referred to it often while drafting documents upon which this country was founded. However, we also know it to be fact that many of these same founding fathers were highly involved in esoteric societies such as the Freemasonry, Rosicrucianism, the Illuminati, and others. They all share a common thread, and that common thread is the direct worship of Satan, believing him to be Lucifer, the god who will save this planet. Those who have been found to be trustworthy are granted the privilege to share in the knowledge of the esoteric.

Now of course, this is difficult for some to believe because no one wants to acknowledge that leaders or founders of any country (much less the United States) could have been heavily involved *in* and indoctrinated *by* esoteric belief systems. How *could* they be if this country was founded upon *Christian* principles?

There are any number of books out today that detail the history of this country, the peculiar physical layout of Washington, D.C., and the fact that people like George Washington used their power and prestige as 33rd Degree Masons to direct this country toward secretly revealed occult prophetic ends. Those prophetic ends are *not* the ends that are disclosed in the Bible, but are those disclosed by Satan himself throughout generations.

Tom Horn's latest book, *Petrus Romanus,* goes into great detail regarding the founders of the United States and how they mapped Washington, D.C., along with the particular reasons why this nation was begun at all. Their involvement in the mystery religions is not unknown, and these secret societies have always seen the United States as the *New Atlantis*, from which a new world order would rise. That has always been the plan, which makes it even more disconcerting to hear people say that if only America would repent and return to her founding roots, God would once again bless her.

If it is true that this country was founded for the sole purpose of being the next Atlantis, it is clear that the God of the Bible was never in the picture from the beginning. Through the use of deceptive language, Satan merely masqueraded as the God of the Bible, causing people to believe that this nation began as a Christian one, offering freedom and sanctuary from the claustrophobic Church of England and injustices encountered throughout Europe. However, it is just as clear that the leaders who brought this country to fruition had a clear understanding of what lay in store and actively engaged in bringing that agenda to the fore.

Consider this from Freemason David Ovason who tells us *"that when the cornerstone of the US Capitol building was laid, it was done through Masonic ritual meant to procure* **approval of the pagan gods***. As recorded in two bronze panels on the Senate doors of the Capitol, George Washington is seen standing in front of a Mason who holds two versions of the Masonic square, while he, himself, uses a Ma-*

sonic trowel on the cornerstone. The apron Washington so famously wore that day bears specific Masonic symbolism...designed to please the 'invisible agencies' who watched over the event,"[22] (Emphasis in original).

In fact, the entire layout of Washington, D.C. was carefully overseen by many who drafted the founding documents for the creation of America.

> *"As many as forty-four (though probably a lower number) of the fifty-six signers of the Declaration of Independence were Freemasons dedicated to the secret destiny of America as the New Atlantis. Numerous US presidents were part of this Craft...That these Rosicrucian-Masonic brothers engineered the US city named after America's first president according to an occult design is indisputable today."*[23]

Horn offers the following as well, as he continues to direct our attention to the actual facts surrounding the founding of America and the physical creation of its capital city:

> *"For those unfamiliar with this secret American-Masonic history, involvement by Freemasons in the development of early America and the symbolic layout of Washington, DC as the capital for the New Atlantis has been so well-documented over the last two decades that even most Masons have ceased denying the affiliation."*[24]

Even while not denying what the founders of this country had in mind, *"most [Masons] vigorously deny that the talisman-like street designs, government buildings, and Masonic monuments were meant for what researcher David Bay calls an 'electric-type grid' that pulsates*

---

[22] Thomas Horn & Chris Putnam, *Petrus Romanus* (Defender, 2012), 419
[23] Ibid, 416-417
[24] Thomas Horn & Chris Putnam, *Petrus Romanus* (Defender, 2012), 417

'with Luciferic power twenty-four hours a day, seven days a week.' Notwithstanding this denial, the government's own records explain otherwise, clearly stating that the capital city's design was 'shepherded' by those who wanted it to reflect dedication to those ancient 'pagan gods' that Bacon and his followers sought wisdom from. "[25]

It would seem that everything connected to the creation of Washington, D.C. was done to please *pagan* gods – Satan himself who, along with many who serve him in the spiritual realms, has masqueraded as various pagan deities throughout history. According to Ovason, *"the dedication of the US Capitol building cornerstone in particular had to be done at a certain astrological time related to the zodiacal constellation Virgo (Isis), while Jupiter was rising in Scorpio, because 'the cornerstone ceremonial was designed not only to gain the approval of the spiritual beings, but also to ensure that these were content that the building was being brought into the world at the right time.'"*[26]

If it is true that the United States was designed to be the harbinger of the next age (or new world order) this alone means that America has been thoroughly steeped in the esoteric even *before* it began. This is the real tragedy, and it is only likely that God blessed anyone in this country because of their individual commitment to Jesus, in spite of those who were using occult sleight of hand to bring forth the powers of darkness. There are members of existing groups of Satanists that attest to the fact that their *craft* has been handed down to them from people in Colonial America and Europe before that.

As we have seen from our quotes from Tom Horn's *Petrus Romanus*, it too often seems that people have been taught that in order to gain power *from* Lucifer and his dark kingdom, certain things had to be done on a certain day, or at a specific location on earth, or when certain stars aligned perfectly. The interest in these things – these mys-

---

[25] Ibid, 418
[26] Thomas Horn & Chris Putnam, *Petrus Romanus* (Defender, 2012), 420

tery religions – have caused many to believe that by following prescribed formulae, these spirits or gods will bless specific events *given* to them, or that the events were designed with their leadership and oversight in mind.

In other words, these believers in the occult fully recognize that as they gain spiritual insight into the esoteric, certain mysteries (gnosis) are revealed to them. Their obligation then is to follow the pattern, or recipe, if you will, that was provided in order to bring certain things to pass. In this way, they come to believe that they have gained deep understanding into the dark halls of occultism and that gives them power over others and power to change the course of future history. Because of that knowledge, they gain a special relationship with those beings of other dimensions that are merely using human beings to accomplish their goals for this nation and this planet. Human beings submit their will in service to these "gods," and in return, they are granted access to higher understanding.

After all, these initiates will tell you that Lucifer is the one who really cares for humanity. He is the one who offers true knowledge allowing man to create a better world. The God of the Bible is actually the One who wants to keep mankind from knowing the truth. In essence then, to the esoteric adherent, Lucifer, not God in Christ, is man's savior.

But what if Satan simply created a thoroughly convoluted process by which human beings could be sucked into thinking that the more they uncovered, the more real truth they actually discovered? What if these same people came to believe that given a certain set of circumstances and their power over those circumstances, they would in turn be able to control powers and principalities so that they could eventually release the dark lord onto this earth in order for *his* will to be done?

In other words, just as Christians partner with God in order that His will be done in and through us, so also has Satan created a very complex system whereby humans are invited to come to him, submit to his lordship and power over them, and they, in return for their subservience, gain *immeasurable insight* into the mysteries of the universe and power to bring those mysteries forth. The revelation of these mysteries does not even have to be *truthful*. As long as people gain something (whether true or not) from their hard work and submission to Satan they will feel compelled to continue to act on Satan's behalf.

People who bow to the true God of the universe through Jesus Christ enter into a life where they are constantly asked and expected to give up their own wants and desires in favor of God's. The result of this is a greater and growing reflection of the character of Jesus in all things, especially in the ability to love God and our fellow human beings.

People who bow to Satan give up the belief that the God of the Bible is the only way, the truth, and the life. This is very easy for unbelievers to do because they are already there. Satan does not expect nor ask his unknowing followers to love one another. In fact, he often promotes a greater sense of selfishness among those who follow him, which is why those most dedicated to him are often exceedingly rich beyond measure. Satan knows how to please in order to keep his followers from running away. Yet does it satisfy? Obviously not.

Please understand what I'm saying. I fully believe that Satan exerts his control over much of what happens on this planet through his ever-present and God-allowed dominion in the spiritual realm above the earth (Ephesians 6) and in those who are already disobedient (unbelievers). People become the willing – though often fully blinded – channels through which Satan releases greater depths of his power onto the physical realm of this planet.

If Satan simply crashed through every open door that he found, forcing his presence where he had not been previously invited, he would soon be seen for what he is: a usurper and evil king of the underworld. That would terrify the average person. Instead, would he not benefit far more by creating a system dressed up as "light" and "truth" that he could effectively dangle in front of people so that they would *willingly* and eventually even with *abandon* open doors wide so that he would become the *invited* guest into a person's life? Would this plan not work far better for him and his minions? At the highest levels of government and control, I believe that this is exactly what Satan does, and he does it well. Because he is the god of this world, he has every right to do that too. He already controls the heart of the lost and will use the unbeliever for his advantage.

Of course, in order to accomplish something of this nature, he must present himself as something he is not: *an angel of light* who comes to this realm for the express purpose of allegedly spreading *truth*. Satan comes to grant insight into the alleged deep mysteries of the secretive realms, realms God says remain off limits to us. These revealed mysteries are fairly *impersonal*, unlike the truth of the gospel of Jesus which is highly *personal*. Satan treats and uses people as if they are merely part of the whole, while God treats people as individuals.

Satan gains far more access to human beings by dressing himself up as an alleged beacon of truth. Because of this and due to the nature of his message, he is hardly ever expected or asked to prove the integrity of either himself or his message. He simply presents a message, and because he has created the complex maze ahead of time, he needs only to guide people into *discovering* its secrets through its manifold paths of enlightenment. Their discovery of it results in their belief that the messenger is filled with integrity because of the apparent truth they have discovered, as was indicated they would.

This is very true in the case of many Satanists. I'm going to generalize a bit here, simply because I do not want to point to specific groups that exist within the United States. I don't want to call them by their names, so I will simply group them all together collectively as *Satanists*. Readers need to understand, though, that there are many branches of Satanism that go by a variety of names and have somewhat different belief systems. In the end, the similarities between the groups are what meld them together, and lately there has been an even greater push to coalesce into a unity, as opposed to being divided.

They themselves will make a distinction between what they might call the *lower levels of Satanism* and the higher, evolved levels. The former levels and groups are often made up of immature, selfish individuals who have not recognized the high goals of Satanism. Their concerns are for themselves, not others within the ranks of Satanism. These types of individuals can obviously create problems for more evolved groups and higher ups simply because they are not aware of the true protocol. The latter groups consist of individuals who have come to understand that there are two overarching goals within all of Satanism:

1. *To physically enthrone Satan in this world, and*
2. *To absolutely destroy Christianity*

It is easy to see how these two goals go hand in hand. As Christians, we understand that the Antichrist is going to be Satan's man, installed into his high position by being the devil incarnate. To the higher level Satanist, this is war, and it is a war that they thoroughly believe they will win at any cost. Some members among Satanists boast that members reach into the highest levels of law enforcement and justice systems. Do they? It is impossible to know, but it is also probably true. Why wouldn't it be the case?

But beyond the actual Satanists and members of dark cabals, there are people who are simply involved in what is seen as the innocuous New Age Movement. Many of these individuals involved in the New Age movement are not necessarily steeped in the secrecy of Satanism; nonetheless, they are unknowingly worshiping the same dark power and are doing his bidding because they believe the lies promoted within the New Age. In the end, it really doesn't seem to matter if one is a practicing Satanist or simply a practitioner of New Age arts because in both cases, lies are heard, believed, and fostered.

Satanists do their part to bring about the destruction (or at least the visible eradication) of Christianity, and those within the New Age work for the same thing. The gods, tenets, and teachings might be different from one group to the next, but ultimately, it is imperative for those within Satanism and the New Age to experience an earth without the trappings of Christianity. All other religions are fine, *except* Christianity. At all costs, Christianity must be taken out.

Courtney Brown has produced a video about Jesus and the Crucifixion that goes completely against the truth taught in Scripture. He believes that his understanding of what actually transpired during the Crucifixion is *the* truth, while what is told in the Bible is not.

Brown makes his case sound plausible to the *uninformed*. In essence, Brown believes that Jesus was not crucified, but someone *else* stood in for Him with Jesus having full knowledge of this dupe. Describing this new information, text from the website states, "*Get ready for the most positive, uplifting, and dramatic re-interpretation of Christian thought in over 2,000 years, one based not on blind faith, but on new data, new research into the science of consciousness, and an understanding of quantum physics.*"[27] Moreover, the information is presented as truth that has been allegedly culled due to the use of remote-viewing methodologies.

---

[27] http://www.crucifixionruse.com/ (accessed 05/2012)

Regarding remote-viewing, it is described as *"a controlled and trainable mental process involving psi (or psychic ability). Remote-viewing procedures were originally developed in laboratories funded by the United States military and intelligence services and used for espionage purposes... Remote viewing is normally considered a controlled shifting of awareness that is performed in the normal waking state of consciousness, and it does not typically involve an out-of-body experience, hypnosis, an altered state of consciousness, or channeling."*[28]

It is interesting that people will enter into and believe the results of these methods because they *appear* to be scientific. The problem of course is that there is absolutely no way to verify the truthfulness of the information received. Moreover, it is equally impossible to determine the actual force (or entity) behind the remote-viewing event. It is very much like a master con artist creating the entire con *and* result for the victim. The con artist then guides the person through the process, deftly bringing them to the predesigned end. The rest is left up to the person's (victim's) imagination to fill in the gaps. Because everything appears to square with science, that in and of itself is enough to provide legitimacy and integrity of the experiment.

Because Satan has created the message far ahead of time in detail, based on his own goals, and his revelation of the highest levels of it are kept only for certain individuals who unflinchingly submit themselves to him, it becomes the perfect con, and it will continue to work until the very end of Satan himself. People wind up worshiping Satan, and they believe their reward is far greater than anything the God of the Bible can promise. They believe that through Satan (*Lucifer* to them), they will one day reign with him forever. Eternal life (damnation) is built into the plan that Satan peddles to those who are intrigued enough to follow after him, becoming available to him as their own individual points of light. Often, as in the case of remote-

---

[28] http://www.farsight.org/WhatIsRemoteViewing.html (accessed 05/2012)

viewing methods, Satan conveniently keeps himself well hidden in the shadows so that the *method* used is fully seen as scientific.

Ultimately, Satan needs people to do his bidding because we live in *this* dimensional realm, unlike Satan and his minions who actually live and work mainly in the spiritual realms. They are certainly allowed entry here. That door to America has been open since the beginning and there have been many searchers of the esoteric who have not only continued to prop that door wide open but have helped in opening up new doors as well.

I believe that this is exactly what has transpired since the founding of America, and it continues to this day. What we are seeing is, I believe, the final stages of Satan's plan coming to fruition. In many ways, he has thrown caution to the wind because he knows he has little time left to accomplish all that he set out to do. There is a momentum that has been reached and there is absolutely no turning back because of it. It will only worsen.

We have already discussed just how evil and seemingly lawless the world has become. We have noted, not only in this book, but in others, how creative Satan has been to insist on controlling the workings of this planet, all the while allowing puny human beings to believe that *we* are the ones who control a great deal, merely with the help and guidance of the adept or transcendent beings of light who exist in other dimensions.

Though in the end, he will fail miserably (and has already been defeated because of the cross of Christ), Satan has left as little as possible up to chance. He has carefully crafted a very complex and convoluted message. He has then simply revealed bits of it here, small pieces of it there, and in doing so he has created an overwhelming desire in people to gain *full disclosure*. This is what many live for today.

We all know how this works and feels. Someone says something and then stops short, realizing they've said too much. You urge them to continue but they say they can't because they would betray a secret if they shared anything with you and they wish they had not said anything at all. You continue to gently nudge them, promising that whatever secrets they tell you will go no further.

Eventually, due to your prodding, they give in and share with you information that they had promised never to reveal. You offer your own assurance that you will not pass anything on to anyone else, yet it is not long before you are the one who has said too much to someone else and they in turn do exactly what you did by urging you to share with them the information that you promised to never share with anyone.

We all know how special it feels to be privy to information that is not available to all. It makes us feel superior, privileged, because of the secret *we* know that others do *not*.

This is how Satan tempted Eve, causing her fall, and Adam with her. This is the exact same modus operandi Satan has been using since the beginning, except that the information he shares now is far more ethereal, esoteric, and convoluted than what he shared with Eve. At its root, it's essentially the same thing, yet our enemy, Satan, has crafted a multifaceted path that he uses to reel people in for his nefarious purposes.

Ultimately, Satan needs people on his side. In fact, because of his narcissism, he *demands* it. It does not work when people stand *against* or resist his schemes, which is why he persuades others to persecute Christians who stand against him. Remember, *all* Christians used to be part and parcel of Satan's kingdom but have left it in order to receive eternal life in God's Kingdom. This is another great reason to incite unbelievers to persecute Christians.

Satan needs people to work with him to bring about his desired ends. At the same time, he is obviously shrewd enough to realize that instead of simply passing out the information, it has been far better to make people think that they have to seek very hard to obtain that information. He has created such an appetite within people for this secret knowledge that he has wound up gathering millions of people to himself throughout various generations. Because he dangles the information in front of them instead of simply tossing it out there to anyone who asks, he has ignited a spiritual desire within many that is only fulfilled when they gain greater understanding into the esoteric.

Think of Tom Sawyer and the white picket fence. Who wants to actually do that kind of work – to paint a fence on a hot day – unless you're getting paid for it? Even then, many would likely balk at the idea. But Tom Sawyer was clever enough to realize that if he just asked people to help him, they would turn him down *flat*. He had to make them *want* to paint that fence! He did just that, to his aunt's chagrin. He managed to make his friends yearn for the chance to paint at least part of that fence!

This is what Satan does. He creates first the *secrets* and then the desire to *know* those secret things of the universe. Once he has done both of these things, he then makes people jump through a plethora of hoops in order to gain that knowledge. He makes them work for it because the more they labor for it, the greater they believe the reward will be. It has worked and it has worked magnificently!

So Satan has not only created the desire within people to learn these secrets but has also created all the rules and alleged secret gnosis in the first place. This is Satan's plan of salvation, if you can call it that, because it helps him gain what he believes is the upper hand against God while keeping millions upon millions of souls from ever understanding that the knowledge they seek is often made up of his lies.

Just as Tom Sawyer created a way to get a fence painted without having to do the work himself, Satan has done the same thing with the human race. He has spent thousands of years plying humanity with games, with knowledge, with tricks, and even with promises of deity. He has made it very difficult to gain that impersonal knowledge without first having to reject the way, the truth, and the life.

People who chase after the dream of "knowing" and being part of the great spiritual drama that allegedly brings Lucifer's man (Antichrist) to the forefront of humanity to lead this world into a new world order indulge in every evil imaginable. They are merely *reflecting* the character of their god, who is thoroughly and unquenchably evil.

Chapter 12
Christian, What Should You Do?

It is accurate to say that evil is overtaking this world at an unprecedented pace, but in truth, ever since the fall of humanity, the world has been an evil place. By the time we reach Genesis chapter nine, we learn that God had decreed that all but Noah and his immediate family (and the animals) would survive a total global flood, in which everything not inside Noah's Ark would *die*. The world had become unquestionably and unquenchably evil. God knew this would occur, but His plan of redemption would still move forward, and it would do so *with* and *through* Noah.

Only a few chapters later in Genesis, we learn that life had become once again so bad that it required God to step in for a bit of surgery. This time, instead of destroying humanity as He had done during Noah's day, the Lord opted to separate humanity into groups by introducing many different cultures and languages into the mix. Up to this point, the world spoke one language and was quickly coming together under the charismatic leadership of Nimrod to build a tower that would reach the heavens (Genesis 11).

God of course knew – and stated as much – that if He allowed men and women to do what they planned, nothing would be beyond their reach. God did what He did to ensure the survival of humanity and further His plan of *redemption*.

Roughly 2,000 years ago, Jesus lived His physical, sinless life, born of a virgin. His perfect life culminated in the painful, barbarous death on a cross, though because of His perfection, death could not keep Him and He rose on the third day.

When that happened, He proved He was worthy to receive and open the seven-sealed scroll of Revelation 5. It is this very scroll that represents the title deed to earth. The judgments contained therein (seven seals, seven trumpets, and seven bowls) will be poured out onto the earth as God's judgment for the way Gentile nations have treated Israel and to purge the final group of rebels from Israel so that God will have His final Jewish Remnant.

Yes, the world is a very evil place, filled with heartache, tears, and terrors. Yet there are some beautiful things in this world as well because it is *still* God's Creation. Satan has control of many things, but his control is on borrowed time. One day – and that day may be sooner than we think – Satan will reap the rewards, not only for his own evil, but for all the evil he has unleashed onto this planet that was created by God. I believe we are living in that time when evil is becoming *extraordinarily* evil.

But as a Christian – if you are *authentically* saved – the question becomes, *what do you do about it?* What should your demeanor be as you move from day to day in this world?

It would be easy to either cave into the demands of the world or to want to run and hide from them. It would also be extremely easy to take personally the attacks meted out by the world to Christians.

Recently, speaker Dan Savage (known for his anti-bullying message) took the time to antagonize young people and especially Christians in a conference on, of all things, anti-bullying.

> *"As many as 100 high school students walked out of a national journalism conference after an anti-bullying speaker began cursing, attacked the Bible and reportedly called those who refused to listen to his rant 'pansy a**es.'*
>
> *"The speaker was Dan Savage, founder of the "It Gets Better" project, an anti-bullying campaign that has reached more than 40 million viewers with contributors ranging from President Obama to Hollywood stars. Savage also writes a sex advice column called 'Savage Love'."*[29]

This type of attitude is becoming the norm that Christians are on the receiving end of, and we wonder how people can be so filled with such *loathing* and *contempt*. We are unable to answer until we look *beyond* the people to the real culprit who deigns to remain in the deep shadows, and that is *Satan*. This world simply mirrors the character and attitude of the ruler of this age.

---

[29] http://radio.foxnews.com/toddstarnes/top-stories/anti-bullying-speaker-curses-mocks-christian-teens.html (accessed 04/27/2012)

Once we shift our focus to him, it all comes into stark focus. Satan does his best work from the shadows, with most believing that he does not exist. He is more than willing to allow those who prefer to deny his existence to continue to do so because it makes his job far easier.

It really doesn't matter what the situation is because wherever there is terror, hatred, injustice, and the like, it is too easy to put a human face to it, rather than to look beyond to the entity that works and plays among the dimensional dark recesses.

Who Pulls the Strings?
So again, what should a Christian's attitude and response be as the world spins seemingly out of control all around us? The first and most important step is to understand who is pulling the strings. We must train ourselves to recognize that though human beings actually and physically create problems this world faces, in most cases, they are little more than puppets (though fully culpable for their actions, words, and thoughts). Sometimes, they are merely giving into their own sin nature as well.

For a long while now, I've believed that people like George Soros are the puppeteers to any number of politicians in Washington. However, the truth of the matter is that Soros himself is a puppet being put to evil use by the master puppeteer of the dark realm. Unless he turns to Christ, Soros will of course be held accountable for everything he does, just as Judas Iscariot was accountable for what he did.

The larger truth, though, is that Soros was given power and ability and amassed a fortune through the misfortunes of others. There was a tremendous miscarriage of justice in what he did, and he is even proud of it. He used those things to do what he has been busy doing for years, and whether it's bringing a bank to its knees or overthrowing a country, the reality is that he does what he does because of the power that is behind him, the very power he willingly gave himself to years ago.[30]

As Christians, we need to be secure in our knowledge and understanding that Satan, while remaining deep undercover, has the real authority and power that he shares with willing (and even unwilling) human beings in order to bring his goals to completion. We need to grasp this because when we do, it makes it far easier to *forgive* and *move on* when God allows bad things to happen to us or our families. Having this understanding grants us the ability to see God's hand in each situation and it makes it so much easier for the desire for personal vengeance to be set aside.

If we take our cue from the apostle Paul, it becomes clear that this was *his* motivation.

> *"Now I want you to know, brethren, that my circumstances have turned out for the greater progress of the gospel, so that my imprisonment in the cause of Christ has become well known throughout the whole praetorian guard and to everyone else, and that most of the brethren, trusting in the Lord because of my imprisonment, have far more courage to speak the word of God without fear"* (Philippians 1:12-14).

In these words from Paul, we see that he understands *why* he is in jail. Rather than complain about it and find fault, he knew that his incarceration was directed by God Himself with Satan as God's puppet to accomplish greater things for the gospel. Through it, as he notes, many brethren became bolder in speaking the truth without fearing the results. Beyond this, imagine how many lives Paul touched with the gospel while in prison who might not have heard the gospel otherwise. He was often chained to soldiers throughout the day. I'm sure he used the opportunity to evangelize them.

---

[30] http://www.thehotjoints.com/2010/09/07/george-soros-not-sorry-he-helped-nazis-kill-his-fellow-jews-in-wwii/

I cannot speak from personal experience, but others who have endured actual physical persecution have spoken of how much easier it was for them to trust God and to speak the truth in love once they came to understand that their situation was ultimately directed by God Himself. He certainly may have used Satan to accomplish it, just as He did with Job and many others in Scripture.

Praying and Praising

We also need to learn to *pray* more. In a recent book I wrote called *Prayer: Exchanging Your Will for God's*, I highlighted prayer itself as taught by Jesus, Paul, James, and others from His Word. We need to become far better at praying, and praying is not simply presenting *my* requests to God, though that is often part of it.

Prayer is doing exactly what the byline stated: *Exchanging Your Will for God's*. The Christian who is serious about following Jesus, worshiping Him, and living a life that honors Him must be serious about prayer. It is through prayer that we learn what the Lord's will is for our life, and it is through prayer that we give up any hold we may have for the various aspects of our life. In essence, if we take our relationship with Jesus seriously, we will want to not only do His will, but we will want to see things from *His* perspective. We must be people who pray and commune with God.

We must also learn to praise Him in all situations.

> *"We urge you, brethren, admonish the unruly, encourage the fainthearted, help the weak, be patient with everyone. See that no one repays another with evil for evil, but always seek after that which is good for one another and for all people. Rejoice always; pray without ceasing; in everything give thanks; for this is God's will for you in Christ Jesus"* (1 Thessalonians 5:14-18).

The verses just quoted do not only say to praise Him in all things. They tell us how to *act*. We should *admonish the unruly, encourage the fainthearted, help the weak, be patient with everyone*, and more. We are *not* to repay evil for evil, and we should always seek good for the other person.

It is not easy being an authentic Christian and sometimes reading words like these proves to us just how difficult living the life of an authentic Christian can be. Yes, we will fail at times, but the overriding concern in our life should be to live a life that pleases God at every turn. When we fail, we should quickly get back up, dust ourselves off, confess our sin, and move on! That also brings Him glory.

The Bible has made it abundantly clear that life is going to become very difficult in these last days. If you are a person who does not put much faith in the area of prophetic discourse, then you may not share that opinion. I would urge you to search the Scriptures so that you can gain an accurate understanding of where this planet is headed.

I believe that Jesus is coming again, that He will one day step out of the third heaven and return to this earth, *physically*. At that point, He will immediately begin judgment (Sheep and the Goats of Matthew 25:31-46) and move to set up His Millennial Kingdom. I believe that according to the Scriptures, He will rule physically for 1,000 years as prophesied in Revelation 20:4-6. In fact, there are many sections of Scripture which speak of the fact that Jesus will physically reign on this planet (Isaiah 9; Ezekiel 37, 43; Zechariah 2, 8; Daniel 7, and *many* others). It is a difficult subject to ignore because it is written about so often by so many in His Word. What do *you* think of it? Do you view it as allegory or a literal event? Better be sure.

It is because I believe that Jesus is returning again to the very planet that He created that I endeavor to live my life in a way that will bring glory to Him. In fact, I believe that the Rapture will occur prior to the Tribulation. While some accuse me of believing in escapism, the truth of the matter is that it causes me to yearn for His return, and if I am yearning for His return, I am hopefully willing and able to share the reason for the hope I have with those who have no hope.

Persecution Happens

I cannot imagine what life was like for the Christian under Nero or during WWI for the Jew. In fact, whenever I hear of some ethnicity involved in "ethnic cleansing," my jaw tightens and I get a really sick feeling in my gut.

I find it difficult to wrap my brain around the horrors that were associated with Nero's reign and the hatred he had for Christians, or Hitler's for the Jews, or radical Muslims for their hatred of anyone who is not Islamic. In Nero's case, blaming Christians for a fire he likely started may have appeased the Romans because they now had their scapegoat, but the utter horror of having to live under the brutal hand of a madman who created tremendous hardships for Christians is something that few Christians today can imagine.

Think about how many of our brothers and sisters died terribly painful deaths under Nero. Hundreds of thousands of Christians were brutally murdered via crucifixion and/or by being used as torches to provide light in his gardens. Christians have suffered in nearly every age since Jesus left this planet, and the promise of suffering has always followed us because the world hates Christians due to the fact that the current overseer hates Jesus. It is happening now in Egypt and other parts of the world.

If we simply focus on these things, we may become immobilized. We will stop dead in our tracks, moving neither to the right, the left, or forward. We cannot allow that to happen.

Regardless of what happens to us or our loved ones, we should continue to move *forward*. We may find that extremely difficult to do at times, yet what is the alternative?

As noted, it is incredibly easy to become hemmed in on all sides if we focus on the terrible things that happen in this life. It can literally cause us to freeze in our steps, but we cannot allow it. I wish I could say that I am perfect at this, but I'm not. There are times when the problems of this world feel as though they are overshadowing my relationship with the Lord. When that happens, the only real option is to continue moving even if I do not feel like or fully understand it.

His Word and Our Faith
It should go without saying, but we all need to be reminded that reading His Word is the way to chase away the devil. Oh, he may stick around for a while to try to get us to sidestep God's Word and God's rule in our life, but if we persevere, Satan will eventually give up...for a time. He'll be back, and we must resist him then as well.

Just reading His Word for understanding is a great thing to do, but eventually, you will want to begin studying a specific book to learn some really great and important truths about God and how He has chosen to work in this world. If we do not read His Word, it's like trying to start a car that has no gas. The engine may try to turn over, but it has no ability to start.

Faith is one of those things that is often nebulous to many of us, myself included. Just exactly what is it all about? According to the writer of Hebrews, we are told, "*Now faith is the assurance of things hoped for, the conviction of things not seen*" (Hebrews 11:1). How do you describe it any better than that?

Faith allows us to see *with* conviction the things that have not yet been fully revealed. We have faith in God that our salvation is not simply a pie in the sky philosophy but a fact that is indisputable. It is because of this that we look forward to the day when we shall see Him and will be like Him (cf. 1 John 3:2-3). In other words, what we have now is *faith*, but one day our faith will become *sight*. At that point, faith will no longer be necessary.

Faith helps us through the difficult times, but just as importantly, it helps us through the good times, the times when we think we've got it all together and are simply relying on ourselves to carry us through. We need faith all the time. Other things we don't need but *think* we do.

For a while there, I would go my favorite social network site and electronically mingle with people of like minds. Sometimes they would post a comment or video and others like me would respond to it. Sometimes I would post a comment or reference a video that meant something to me and others would comment on it.

The problem with any social network is that it is easy to become hooked on it. Before you realize what's transpired, you have spent a good portion of your day mingling with others, and at the end of the day you have to wonder what, if anything, you have actually accomplished.

Added to this is the fact that many things that people discuss are often conspiratorial in nature, and because of that things can get a bit sideways. Who really knows the truth behind the many alleged conspiracy theories out there today? Some of them may not even be conspiratorial in nature necessarily. Maybe they are designed to provoke fear in a person, a fear that prompts the person to feel like something needs to be done *now* in order to stave off some life-threatening situation that will affect the entire world if something is not done.

Have *you* ever spent time on one of the social networks on the Internet? Social networks can be great time wasters. I have often thought about discontinuing any type of a presence on my favorite social network. Would I be better off without it? Except for staying in touch with friends and loved ones, the answer is *probably*.

Authentic Christians need to realize that God has only given us this one life to live. It has been written that God has a plan for our life and Satan has a plan for our life as well. We need to understand that and pray that as we go through each day. God will gain the victory as we submit ourselves to Him. If we do not submit to Him, we have already submitted to the enemy.

It's About Evangelism and Glorifying God
In truth, our job is bringing glory to God every moment of every day. That said, we also need to understand that being perfect is not something we will be able to attain in this life. Still, even in our failures we can ultimately bring glory to God through our confession and our determination to get back on the correct path.

Bringing God glory is all about dying to self and submitting ourselves to His will. Ultimately, our life should be a witness to everyone we meet because, as someone has said, our life may be the only Bible some people read.

If glorifying God is our primary purpose, *evangelism* should be the way there because every time someone comes to know Jesus as Savior and Lord, another soul is removed from the kingdom of darkness and placed into God's Kingdom of glorious light. If we are focused on ourselves and our problems, it is difficult to see the need to evangelize. Sometimes, those who hurt us are in desperate need of Jesus. If we harbor a grudge because we do not recognize that Satan is the instigator, that will keep us from living a life of testimony for God.

Recently, we as a family participated in a food packing event promoted by Feed the Hungry (feedthehungry.org). For this event, you pay for the privilege of buying and packaging food that is sent to a variety of places around this planet, places like Haiti, Kenya, Jamaica, and many others.

The process goes like this: a group of people gather around tables put together in the shape of a U. The process starts with one person placing a bag under a funnel. Measured amounts of food – vitamins, soy, vegetables, and rice – are placed in the bag as it moves along the assembly line process. Finally, the open end of the bag is hermetically sealed.

When forty of these bags are placed on the table at the end, they are then all taken and placed neatly in a cardboard box. Once all forty are inside the box, that box is sealed and taken to a pallet where it joins other boxes. Once there are enough sealed boxes on that pallet, the pallet itself is wrapped with plastic wrap to hold it together and then it is removed by truck along with many other pallets to head to a cargo plane. Many pallets are then transported to a variety of foreign countries in order to feed children.

The contents of each bag – the vitamin powder, soy, vegetables, and rice – are specifically designed to bring children *back* from starvation. It not only reverses the process but begins building their tiny bodies so that they become healthy.

The goal of Feed the Hungry is simple: *to supply nutritious, daily meals to vulnerable children living in the world's least developed nations. Children also receive an education that gives them hope for the future.*[31]

Ultimately, the goal is to create healthy, educated children who learn about Jesus, become authentic Christians, and then turn around and learn to make disciples of others. Is it any wonder that Jesus took the time to feed people when such large crowds gathered? He wasn't simply using His deity to solve a hunger problem. He obviously knew that people who were fed and satisfied were able to hear the message far better than those who went hungry.

---

[31] http://www.feedthehungry.org/Who-We-Are/Are.cfm (accessed 05/05/2012)

As Christians it is our obligation to do what we can to feed and clothe those who are in dire need. But we certainly cannot stop there. We must go past ministering to a person's physical needs and engage their spiritual needs as well. To only feed or clothe someone might stave off death by starvation, but spiritually, they are still *dead!*

Isn't it ironic how often people become enamored with the many miracles that Jesus performed, thinking that they wish they could do those same miracles in the same way today? Many believe that if there are no supernatural miracles in your life, you are doing something wrong as a believer. That's garbage. We *have* the ability to feed the hungry and clothe the naked, and even though it is often done today in a very pedestrian or mundane way, it is no less a miracle.

We need to see the need! We need to understand that the evangelistic need is tremendously great! But too often we become sidetracked into thinking that we must feed our own "5,000" just like Jesus did and if we can't do it that way, then we are failures. That's exactly what Satan would like us to think. If he isn't getting us to focus on our problems, which often come to us because of other human beings, he wants us to lose sight of the true goal of evangelizing by causing us to focus on the *way* Jesus evangelized, instead of simply meeting the need that exists.

Some of these children in these foreign countries have some amazing stories. We learned of one young boy who came to a school in Kenya after witnessing his entire family slaughtered by factions. He survived and became part of the school run by Christians who eventually brought him back from starvation to health, to learning, and he now has the desire to go back to his home area as a pastor to those people who killed his family members. How does this happen? He could have focused on the fact that specific individuals took the lives of those he loved. Instead, by God's grace and the miracle of a food pack-a-thon, he was not only restored to health, but became educated *and* became an authentic believer who wants nothing more than to share the love of God that was shared with him! That is a miracle that brings glory to God!

I can tell you firsthand what a blessing it was to be part of that Feed the Hungry pack-a-thon! We are not done yet, because if the Lord leads, we want to personally go to one of these countries to pass out the food and hopefully be a blessing to those people. One box of food (forty bags) is enough to feed one child for an entire school year. It is something that nearly anyone can be involved in so that people will learn that God cares, He loves, and He has salvation for all who ask.

If we understood – *really* understood – and believed that Satan is behind problems in our lives, it would be far easier for us to forgive people and move on. This does not mean that God does not allow bad things to happen in our life. It means that while He *does* allow the devil to unleash on us from time to time, He has a purpose in allowing those things to come our way. His purposes are always meant to bring Him glory.

James tells us to "*[c]onsider it all joy, my brethren, when you encounter various trials, knowing that the testing of your faith produces endurance. And let endurance have its perfect result, so that you may be perfect and complete, lacking in nothing*" (James 1:2-4). This is important to understand, but very difficult to put into practice. Who wants to praise God when bad things happen? I doubt if Joseph's first reaction after being accused by Potiphar's wife of attempted rape was *joy* (cf. Genesis 39)! We know that Joseph cried loudly when he understood that his brothers were going to sell him as a slave (cf. Genesis 37; see also 42:21). He reacted humanly to bad things, but over the years, God taught him some very valuable lessons, and he learned to appreciate what God had done.

James' words above seem like the ravings of a lunatic. Who delights in bad things? But the truth is that when we praise God for things that we consider to be bad in our life, we are actually *releasing* them:

giving them up to God. We are recognizing that we are slaves to God, and as such, He has a right to do whatever He wants with us.

In James 1:13-17, we read the following words, as a follow-up to the ones above where James tells us to rejoice in various trials:

> *"Let no one say when he is tempted, 'I am being tempted by God'; for God cannot be tempted by evil, and He Himself does not tempt anyone. But each one is tempted when he is carried away and enticed by his own lust. Then when lust has conceived, it gives birth to sin; and when sin is accomplished, it brings forth death. Do not be deceived, my beloved brethren. Every good thing given and every perfect gift is from above, coming down from the Father of lights, with whom there is no variation or shifting shadow."*

James is making it very clear that when bad things happen to us, God isn't sending those things. Satan is doing that. However, it is also clear that God is *allowing* them to come our way so that we will learn to endure and endurance will have its perfect work. In other words, trials will cause us to grow in our faith, if we allow them to do so.

However, if we focus on the *individual* that Satan is using to bring the trial our way, then it will become far more difficult to offer praise for it (Let's not forget that God Himself will use people to persecute us as well!). We will tend to want to focus on the *person* that the trial is coming to us *through* instead of understanding that God has allowed the situation for our own good and growth and ultimately for His glory.

Judas betrayed our Lord. Jesus knew it would happen. I do not believe for one moment that Jesus held a grudge against Judas. I do not believe He focused on Judas. I fully believe that Jesus understood completely that Judas was merely a pawn in Satan's plan. Once Satan was done with Judas and Judas was left to himself to realize what he had done, he chose to end his own life because he could not stand the reality of that horror that he had been part of where Jesus was concerned.

Jesus loved Judas as He loves all people. Yes, Jesus said that it would have been better for Judas had he not been born (cf. Matthew 26:24), but that is because He also knew Judas would never repent and would spend eternity in hell because of his *lack* of repentance. It is that simple *and* profound.

Folks, as Christians – if you *are* an authentic Christian – we need to be about the Father's will just as Jesus was about the Father's will. It should not matter how evil life becomes or seems to become. Whether in good times or in bad times, we should yearn to fulfill God's will for our lives. That is what authentic Christians should do and there is no room for debating it. We *must* be about the Father's will in this evil age, and our overarching concern should be to see a growing number of people exiting Satan's kingdom because they are receiving salvation.

The book of Revelation offers us tremendous insight into the things that this world will experience during the days leading up to and including the period known as the Tribulation. Whether you believe in the Tribulation or not, reading God's Word should prove to you that this world is not going to get better until perfection reigns. If anything, the evil that men and women do will increase among people and throughout the world on a steady basis as we move toward the end (2 Timothy 3:13). If you don't believe that, then you are saying that Paul is a liar and God's Word cannot be trusted. God is not done working to take more people out of the kingdom of darkness, and because of that, authentic Christians need to be busy spreading the gospel of Jesus and meeting the physical needs of people who are in want.

Folks, I pray that the Lord will bless you and keep you. I pray that He will guide you through all the darkness that this world has to offer. He *will* see you through. He *will* uphold you with His righteous right hand.

Evil is as evil does. It can do nothing different. You can pretend it doesn't exist or that it is not as bad as it appears to be. You can believe that if you simply change society, then people will change as a result and because of that belief spend your days doing whatever you can to affect change. You can do these things or you can choose to become thoroughly immersed in the process of evangelizing the lost. In this way, you will grow closer to the Lord, recognizing that nothing comes your way without His approval.

Without a doubt, people are going to become even worse than they are now. All that means is that the devil knows his time is short. In the meantime, souls need to be saved. People need to come to know that Jesus is alive and that He died for them. People need the Lord, and if we do not tell them – by our words, our actions, our very life – who will?

Chapter 13
Behind Enemy Lines

Saving the hostages. It's what it's all about. In every war or police action in which special agents are commissioned to go into a zone for the sole purpose of rescuing others, it can be harrowing. Yet that is the job brave men and women are called upon to do. They know it. They understand the risks involved, and in spite of those risks, something compels them to do what the average person cannot do.

Because of one of the most recent military events that occurred roughly a year ago, in which a team of SEALs were sent into Afghanistan on a secret mission to capture bin Laden, we understand as an observer many of the risks involved and ultimately what is at stake. In this case, a group of elite, trained operatives were literally sent behind enemy lines to conduct a mission that was to result in the death or capture of bin Laden, the world's most wanted terrorist. The world knows what happened, at least as far as the outcome is concerned.

The SEAL team surreptitiously stormed bin Laden's hideout, cornered and killed him, then captured his dead body. This was the result of long hours of planning, and in the end there was victory because the job was done and done well.

We've all watched movies or TV programs in which a hostage situation exists and special teams of highly trained individuals are called upon to do what they have been trained to do. Their job is to go into that dangerous situation and, keeping causalities to a minimum, save those people who are being held captive, while arresting or killing the hostage-taker. We understand how it works.

Consider the military men and women who go to another country to fight for either the freedom of that particular country or to guard the freedoms that exist in another one. Their job is to be always on the alert for the enemy and to literally encroach upon the enemy territory while at the same time not be taken down by that enemy.

A perfect example of this type of bravery in battle is found in the person of Captain Ed "Too Tall" Freeman. I received an email one day which contained information about a gentleman named Ed Freeman. After reading the story, I did some research and found that numerous online sites verify its authenticity. However, it also needs to be stated that the information has been used as critical fodder against the high- profile lives of certain celebrities who seem to gain and keep the world's attention while people like Freeman remain steadfastly in the background.

> *You're a 19 year old kid. You're critically wounded and dying in the jungle somewhere in the Central Highlands of Viet Nam. It's November 11, 1967.*
>
> *Your unit is outnumbered 8-1 and the enemy fire is so intense from 100 yards away, that your CO (commanding officer) has ordered the helicopters to stop coming in.*
>
> *You're lying there, listening to the enemy machine guns and you know you're not getting out. Your family is half way around the world, 12,000 miles away, and you'll never see them again.*
>
> *As the world starts to fade in and out, you know this is the day. Then - over the machine gun noise - you faintly hear that sound of a helicopter.*
>
> *You look up to see a Huey coming in. But, it doesn't seem real because no MedEvac markings are on it.*
>
> *Captain Ed Freeman is coming in for you.*
>
> *He's not MedEvac so it's not his job, but he heard the radio call and decided he's flying his Huey down into the machine gun fire anyway, even after the MedEvacs were ordered not to come. He's coming anyway.*
>
> *He drops it in and sits there in the machine gun fire, as they load three of you at a time on board. Then he flies you up and out through the gunfire to the doctors and nurses and safety.*
>
> *And, he kept coming back!! Thirteen more times until all the wounded were out. No one knew until the mission was over that the Captain had been hit four times in the legs and left arm.*

He took twenty-nine of you and your buddies out that day. Some would not have made it without the Captain and his Huey.

Medal of Honor Recipient, Captain Ed Freeman, United States Air Force, died last Wednesday (August 20, 2008) at the age of 70, in Boise, Idaho.

The previous story is true and verified. There are photos on the 'Net of Captain Ed Freeman receiving his medal of honor from then President Bush. It is a story worth reading because in many ways, it obliges us to understand that as Christians this is what we are also called to do, even though most of us are not in the military.

If, as authentic Christians, will begin to think of ourselves as we truthfully are, we will gain a far greater understanding of our true mission while we remain on this earth. God wants us to know that once we become authentic Christians, for as long as we remain in this life, we are on-duty soldiers always located *behind enemy lines*. That will never change until the day we are taken out of this life. We need to comprehend this truth not only for our benefit but for the benefit of all of the lost souls alive during our generation.

Picture the soldier dropped in behind enemy lines. He knows his mission, and that mission compels him forward. It might be to go into enemy territory for the sole purpose of evacuating other military personnel, like Captain Freeman. It might be to engage the enemy as cover for a military operation taking place not far away. Ultimately, the purpose of that action is to save the lives of people, whether other military personnel or civilians caught up into the thick of things.

How does a military person fulfill that job without getting sidetracked? How do they continue to carry out their orders in spite of the odds, even if it means they die trying? They do so by keeping one thing in mind. That one thing is realizing for whom they fight.

Military personnel who go behind the lines to carry out a military objective are only good as long as they remember who they represent. Once a serviceman begins to step away from that realization, he can all too quickly begin to entertain thoughts that his operation is not as important as he originally thought.

Imagine if members of the SEAL team that went in after bin Laden had begun to think that they were not that important to the mission or if they became distracted by aspects of life in that area of the world. They would cease to be of benefit to other team members, and that would pose great risk to the operation itself.

You likely know where I'm going with this. It is very easy – in fact, it is *too* easy – for the Christian to become sidetracked because Satan makes aspects of this world seem so palatable. Once the true Christian begins to be persuaded by those things in the world that Satan holds out as glittery trinkets we find mesmerizing, our benefit to ourselves and others is jeopardized. Our allegiance to God begins to crumble.

There are many MIAs related to the Vietnam conflict. According to numerous stories and reports, at least some are believed to be still in areas of Vietnam living their lives as non-military personnel. They have adopted themselves to the language and culture for one reason or another. Because they have become part of the Vietnam culture, they ceased to be part of the United States military.

If it is true that men such as these exist in Vietnam, they likely believe that the choice they made – to remain in Vietnam – is a form of desertion. Whether this is the case or not (and who knows what the specific circumstances might be in each case, including extended torture or what have you that precipitated their going AWOL) these individuals stopped being part of the U.S. military machine. They now live for themselves apart from the military they at one point served.

This could (and does) happen to Christians. We are not exempt from reducing our loyalties or switching them altogether. How can we keep this from happening? I believe if we fully understood the reality of our true citizenship, that alone would be one of the greatest checks to ensure our steadfast allegiance to Jesus and His Kingdom.

There are many places in Scripture where we are taught things about our walk in this world and our citizenship once we become authentic Christians. In Philippians 3:20, Paul informs us that *"our citizenship is in heaven, from which also we eagerly wait for a Savior, the Lord Jesus Christ."*

Why does he tell us this at that point in the epistle to the Philippians? In the earlier portion of this very same chapter, Paul takes the time to warn his readers about those who would try to change the gospel of Jesus, either by *adding* requirements to it or by trying to *reduce* it to something it is not.

Paul explained that though humanly speaking, he at one time thought his credentials might have saved him, in the end, they add nothing to him for salvation. In fact, he states that he counts them as loss for the sake of knowing Christ (cf. Philippians 3:7).

He speaks of having the correct attitude (humility) as we walk through this life so that we might gain more of Jesus. He eventually gets to the point of discussing those who walk as enemies of the cross (v. 18), *"whose end is destruction, whose god is their appetite, and whose glory is in their shame,* **who set their minds on earthly things**" (v. 19; emphasis added). Though these people believe that they are living the correct life, it will end in complete destruction. Their biggest problem is that they are concerned about earthly things, not heavenly ones. The world is filled with unbelievers like this, people who see no need to consider the truth about the afterlife. They live for the here and now, not the tomorrow and eternity. This is what classifies people who do not know the Lord, people who do not have authentic salvation and see no need for it. They believe they are content, and if they are wealthy, they see themselves as having no need for anything. That's the unbeliever in this world compared with the Christian.

However, in John 15, Jesus begins to teach His apostles that even authentic Christians can become thoroughly ineffectual in this life. We can become hampered by the cares of this world. We might become all too concerned about our job, our family, our education, our children and their lives. While there is nothing wrong with making a living and even making plans, it is imperative that we do not look at these things as if we are in charge of creating them and carrying them through. James points out the truth that we must give these things to the Lord for His will to be accomplished (cf. James 4:13-17). It is important to grasp the fact that the things of this world can carry us away from our true mission as authentic Christians.

Jesus refers to Himself as the *Vine* in John 15. He is the Vine and we are the branches. As long as we remain *in Him*, we will bear fruit. What does that mean?

Some commentators believe that Jesus is actually comparing authentic Christians to non-believers. Permit me to disagree. Jesus specifically references those who *abide* in Him, then stop abiding. At first glance, it might appear as though He is actually speaking about someone who winds up *losing* their salvation. I think this is why some commentators attribute His remarks to believers and non-believers.

The problem, though, is that I believe there are too many portions of Scripture that prove that salvation cannot be lost. I've written a book about it and won't take the time to deal with it here.[32] For me then, the question becomes, if Jesus is not talking about actually being able

---

[32] *Finishing the Race*, by Fred DeRuvo, deals with the issue of eternal security.

to lose salvation and He's not talking about the contrast between truly saved and non-believing individuals, what then is He referring to here?

I believe that Jesus is clearly pointing out that the Christian who abides in Him, or remains committed to Him in obedience through the exchange of his or her will for His, will be blessed by bearing fruit. It stands to reason, does it not, that the authentic Christian who lives *for* Jesus willingly submits himself to Him so that His will can be accomplished in and through that Christian? In such a case then, that Christian is actively engaged in allowing God to work in and through his or herself so that God will be glorified. That is supposed to be the natural state and life of each and every believer. However, it is safe to say that many are not so engaged.

Too many Christians start becoming involved in this life to the point that they lose sight of their mission. Like the soldier who fails to remain faithfully devoted to his mission and becomes largely ineffective because of it, the Christian can go through the same thing. This does *not* mean that salvation is lost. It means that glorifying God through bearing fruit is set aside.

The soldier who becomes distracted from his course might wind up causing the entire mission to fail. It is not that he is no longer a soldier. It is that he has begun *acting* as if he is no longer a soldier. If that continues, he may wind up jeopardizing his own involvement in the mission as well as the lives of other soldiers. If this attitude continues during the mission, he could end up making tragic mistakes that could cause his death or someone else's.

I believe Ananias and Sapphira of Acts 5 bear this out. There is no indication that the two were unbelievers, and it certainly appears as though they were, in fact, part of the early church, not merely by being physically present, but spiritually as well. As was the way of the early church, it got to a point where people began to sell what they had and donate their money to the church. People believed that the Lord's return was going to be soon, and because of that they didn't need as much as they had. They also felt an obligation to do what they could to help other brothers and sisters in need.

The problem is that for some reason, these two individuals got together and decided that they would sell their extra parcel of land and give only part of the proceeds to the church. There is nothing wrong with that because they were under no obligation to give anything to the Church originally. The problem existed because they both decided they would lie and pretend that they gave *all* the proceeds, even though they had both agreed to keep back part of the money they made on the deal.

God decided that this was not acceptable and chose to remove them from this life because of this failure to be truthful with God. As Peter tells them, they had lied to the Holy Spirit (cf. Acts 5:3). They had full control over the money they made by selling that land and had they wished they could have given all, part, or nothing to the church. Their choice to give only a portion while trying to make themselves appear as though they had given everything proved to be their undoing.

In 1 Corinthians 11:30, Paul explains to the Corinthian believers that a number of their congregation had become sick and some had even "fallen asleep" (which is another way of saying they died when referencing believers). The reason they died is due to their own sin, and that sin was specifically related to the Lord's Supper, which at least some of the Corinthians did not take seriously. Please take the time to read the entire eleventh chapter of 1 Corinthians.

Getting back to Jesus and John 15, it seems clear to me that Jesus is specifically referring to our blessed position in Christ. As long as we continue to abide in Him by being *obedient to Him*, we will be blessed and bear fruit. We all know how easily we can become bored with aspects of Christianity. We can decide to stop going to church and enjoying fellowship with others. We can stop reading His Word and praying. We can cease to evangelize the lost.

Paul's entire first letter to the Corinthian church highlights the fact that in many ways, those Christians – and they *were* Christians – exemplify people who were extremely immature in Christ. They did little to promote godly living and seemed to care more about arguing and getting drunk than glorifying God.

This is the picture of a Christian who is far more concerned about himself than about Jesus or the lost people of the world. What is the solution to this? The solution is to *abide in Christ*. Again, abiding in Him means to *obey*. Obedience comes through submitting our will to Him. It is what Jesus did every day of His life. We see the perfect example of this in the Garden of Gethsemane, where Jesus greatly struggled to give up His will in exchange for the Father's. He worked through it, even sweating drops of blood because of the intensity of the battle, until He could say "not my will, but yours be done." That is the obedience that God is looking for in each of His children.

If you take the time to look over your life, only you can know how good you are at submitting yourself to Him for His service. Those who do submit to His will are those who abide in Him and because of that, bear fruit.

John 15:6 states, "*If anyone does not abide in Me, he is thrown away as a branch and dries up; and they gather them, and cast them into the fire and they are burned.*" This might seem to suggest that we lose salvation, but I don't see that. We can look to Paul again for clarification here.

1 Corinthians 3:15 notes, "*If any man's work is burned up, he will suffer loss; but he himself will be saved, yet so as through fire.*" Taking these two statements together, it seems clear enough that Jesus and

Paul are saying the same thing, but describing it two different ways. Jesus is saying that if a person continues not abiding in Him, he is taken away from the place of blessing and will be cast in the fire where he will obviously suffer loss. Paul further clarifies this by telling us that the works of all Christians will go through judgment. Only those works that remain after passing through the fire are those that will earn eternal reward. Even here in 1 Corinthians 3, Paul is not talking about a potential loss of salvation. He is speaking of a loss of rewards. Notice he says that the person "will be saved, yet so as through fire." The person will be saved, but their works will be burned up.

I believe that Jesus is speaking of this same thing. If not, then Paul and Jesus are contradicting each other and we know that this cannot occur in Scripture.

As Christians, we need to realize that we are behind enemy lines and our citizenship is in heaven. We cannot allow the cares of this world to distract us from the job at hand, which is the spreading of the gospel. To Timothy, Paul remarks, *"No soldier in active service entangles himself in the affairs of everyday life, so that he may please the one who enlisted him as a soldier"* (2 Timothy 2:4). That soldier would amount to nothing.

Authentic Christians are active soldiers on the duty roster. We must live our lives like this until the day we are called home, and then our active service will be over. For now, living behind enemy lines means that we should be alert to the very real and constant threat of the enemy. While we must always be aware that he can strike at any time, we must also be on our constant guard for those in the enemy's camp that can be rescued. It is a two-pronged mentality that we must live by in order to survive and bring great honor to our Commander.

Not seeing ourselves on active duty makes it difficult to live the life of an authentic Christian. Not realizing that our battle is against entities in the spiritual realm also makes it very difficult. If we focus on people who are used as puppets for Satan's purposes, it is easy to hold a grudge, to withhold love, and to fail to see people as individuals who need Jesus and His salvation. Because we live in the flesh and see others who also live in the flesh, it becomes easy to focus on them and their wrongdoing instead of seeing them as people who need the Lord.

If our citizenship is truly in heaven as the Bible tells us it is, then our main goal should be to want to rescue as many hostages from within Satan's kingdom as possible so that they too will come to know and enjoy a citizenship that is in heaven. This is our goal, and it is when we begin to comprehend the truth that our battle is not against flesh and blood but against powers and principalities in the heavenly realms that we are able to live that goal.

The coming anarchy that collapses the nations will usher in a one-world government, causing it to rise from the ashes. Christians need to stand against that – not to keep it from happening, because it *will* happen. We should stand against it because of the souls that are currently involved in it that need salvation.

We cannot think that we will be able to change this world. The die has been cast. Prophecy is in motion. The things that are going to happen will happen. The difference we can make as authentic Christians is found in capturing those held hostage within Satan's kingdom and introducing them to the King of the Kingdom of Light.

We need to stand up and be counted as part of God's army as He continues to redeem lost souls from Satan's camp. Doing anything less will find us guilty of aiding and abetting the enemy.

Chapter 14
Prayer Warfare

There is not enough that can be said about the power of prayer. It is the greatest weapon that the Christian has at his or her disposal. Unfortunately, it is not used enough. While we Christians use prayer when we are desperate, or to provide God with our personal "wish list," it is likely that we underestimate the value and power of prayer when confronting the enemy and his strongholds.

Consider this: if Satanists will spend years performing all sorts of Magick rituals and participate in Black Masses in order to release the powers of darkness onto this earth, either as territorial spirits or to harass Christians, why are we not using prayer as a means to defend and push back against such demonic activity?

I wrote an article on my blog that highlights what a writer from Canada stated about what may be in store for America this summer. The writer details the information he has from someone he alleges is employed by the Department of Homeland Security. Essentially, as stated in the article, the goal is to create civil war this summer so that Martial Law can be called into existence. If Martial Law comes into play, then it is very likely that the November elections will *not* occur.

Moreover, if Martial Law is called for, that means that major portions of the United States will be dominated by society run amok, more so than we now experience. This could all easily play into Satan's hands so that he might precipitate a total collapse of society in order to bring about a one-world government. If this happens, then the arrival of the Antichrist is not that far into the future.

So what should Christians do upon learning of these alleged plans? Do we opt to work within the political arena to change things? Do we try to fight this governmental overreach by working through our local governments or by writing our state legislators asking them to do what is right? We could do those things and we might get somewhere. However, wouldn't it be far superior to get on our knees and bring this problem *to the Lord*?

Shouldn't we take the time and energy to fight the battle in prayer, asking the Lord to stand against this alleged coming onslaught? I believe we will gain far more ground this way than by using anything in society or the political realm to fight the battle there.

As Christians, we do not have to give up and roll over. We do not have to kowtow to the enemy because we believe that he has plans to take down the United States. At the same time, it may very well be that God will say "no" to our prayers asking him to force the powers of darkness to stand down, but we won't know that until we ask, will we?

As Christians, do we *pray* enough? We need to remember that the reason we should pray is because there are lost souls who yet need to be saved. We pray because as long as the enemy has them in his camp, they will never be truly free, in spite of the fact that they fully believe they have never been freer. Freedom is found only in Christ.

God expects us to use prayer to our advantage, asking God to intervene in the affairs of men often. We are not taking our position as Christians seriously if we are not spending much time in prayer.

Can we pray that God will change the heart of our leaders or remove them from office? You bet. Can we pray that God will protect our home, our family, and our churches from the invasive onslaught of the enemy? Absolutely. He may choose something else, but we can still ask.

We should be people of prayer. We need to be people who pray, and we have to get past the two to three minutes of prayer where we ask God to fulfill our desires for His glory, amen. We need to learn and understand that the enemy never sleeps and the people who serve him take their job seriously.

Think of the prince of Persia in Daniel 10. There was a very real battle going on between the angel that was sent from God's throne and the prince of Persia. That fight lasted twenty-one days, and the angel was only freed to go on his way after Michael the Archangel inserted himself into the mix and overpowered the prince of Persia. It took *three weeks*! That should tell us something: that the fight in the spiritual realm is very real, very dynamic, and those beings play for keeps. What is more interesting is that this very same prince of Persia, who existed during Daniel's day and kept an angel away from Daniel for twenty-one days, *still lives now*. It is the same powerful demon who controls a territory of this world. How many other demons control other parts of the world? We may not be able to pray against them, but at least we know that these battles rage. Certainly, Daniel was not even aware of that particular battle until he was informed of it. Even then, there is no indication that he shifted his prayer focus to the spiritual realms and focused on attempting to defeat the beings that existed and fought there. What happens in the spiritual realms is God's business and He takes care of it. We need to be concerned for the people in our physical realm. They need salvation.

Yet too many of us Christians are enamored with many aspects of this life. We have lost sight of the fact that others are in need of salvation. We are tempted to become complacent, settled, and bogged down by the routine of life. This is not what a good soldier does. A good soldier is always on his guard and always ready to fight.

We are living in a day and age when there is dire need for spiritual discernment. If we ask God to provide us with this type of discernment, He will certainly grant that request. However, it is not in merely *possessing* spiritual discernment that His will is being accomplished. It is in *using* that spiritual discernment in order to stand against the enemy. Ultimately, the goal is *evangelism*. People need to be saved, and Satan and his minions will do whatever they can to keep that from happening. That is their whole purpose, though their stated goal is to enthrone Satan and destroy Christianity. If they could accomplish that, then no one would be able to *leave* Satan's kingdom.

This is what the fight is all about: *people*. Souls hang in the balance. As authentic Christians, we remain here on this earth, behind enemy lines, in order to free the hostages that the devil has captured. It is that simple and the authority we have in Christ is that effective in bringing this to fruition.

If we consider merely one event in the life of Christ, we can see that ultimately, the goal of His redemptive purposes is so that people can receive salvation. Of course, this notion may seem extremely obvious, but too often, Christians become blind to it as we go through life. Too often, Christians are over-involved in political activism to the exclusion of evangelism.

In Mark 5, we read of the situation involving the (likely) Jewish man who was thoroughly possessed. He is known as the The Gerasene Demoniac because he was in that area of the world in the country of Gerasenes. Notice that as soon as Jesus got off the boat and began walking toward the man, something extremely interesting happened: *"Seeing Jesus from a distance, **he ran up and bowed down before Him**; and shouting with a loud voice, he said, 'What business do we have with each other, Jesus, Son of the Most High God? I implore You by God, do not torment me'!"* (Mark 5:6-7; emphasis added)

Please note that the man – though completely possessed by demonic spirits – recognized who Jesus was and understood His authority over him/them. The possessed man proved this by running up to Jesus and *bowing* before Him.

The Bible describes this individual to us: *"And no one was able to bind him anymore, even with a chain; because he had often been bound with shackles and chains, and the chains had been torn apart by him and the shackles broken in pieces, and no one was strong enough to subdue him. Constantly, night and day, he was screaming among the tombs and in the mountains, and gashing himself with stones"* (Mark 5:3-5).

This is tragic. We do not know how the man came to be so engulfed by demon spirits. All we know is that because of it he was relegated to the tombs, which of course for an orthodox Jew would have meant to become unclean. But more than this, the demons exercised such power and strength in and through this man that chains could not hold him and he was easily able to break the shackles that were used on his ankles.

Ultimately, no other person was strong enough for this man, so powerful was he under the dominance of demons. Notice also that he spent his nights and days screaming among the tombs and cutting himself with sharp stones. What a life! Imagine this poor man's sufferings.

Then Jesus comes along, and instead of overpowering Jesus, the many demons in the man implicitly understood that Jesus had power *over* them. All power is gone from them as they *bow* before the God of the universe. No more screaming. No more cutting the man they inhabit with sharp stones. They understand who they are up against and they are no match.

They even beg Jesus not to torment them. But Jesus calls for them to come out of the man, releasing him from their grasp. This son of Israel who, for some reason, has become a habitation of devils is in need of salvation. Jesus casts them out into the pigs nearby as requested. Once free of the demons, the man comes into his right mind (cf. Mark 5:15). The man obviously became saved in the knowledge of Jesus Christ that very day.

Even though the townspeople did not want Jesus to remain in their area (and He complied), the previously demon-possessed man asked that he might go with Jesus. Instead, Jesus told the man to go and tell others what had happened to him: how he had been freed from Satan's hold over him and that he was now in the Kingdom of Light, having been rescued from the kingdom of darkness.

This is our calling: to escort the captive from the enemy's camp to God's camp, and most who find their freedom from the kingdom of darkness do so in a far more mundane way than that described in Mark 5. Are you up for it? Are you ready to move out in God's Name and in His authority in order to release those in bondage in order that they might receive the only true salvation that is available?

Satan wants us to be thoroughly involved in the affairs of the world so that we do not see the needs of those we pass by every day. Satan cannot stop us from becoming Christians, but he can and does work very hard to make us as ineffective as possible in our walk with Christ in this life. That is his goal when another one of his captives escapes his kingdom into Christianity.

We have been given the authority to make disciples of people from all nations. Do we think that Satan will sit idly by as we go about that task? On the contrary, he will do everything within his power to keep us from fulfilling that objective. However, he will never be able to control the authentic Christian or have victory over him. In Christ, we are already victorious and Satan is fully defeated.

Are you clothed in the armor of God and in the power of His might? Satan seeks to stop Christians. He seeks to bind and blind the lost. He also seeks to steal the Word of God from people's hearts (Luke 8). Wherever believers are preaching the gospel of Jesus, Satan or his demons are there trying to thwart our efforts.

As authentic believers, we need to understand that it is the truth of the gospel that saves people from Satan's kingdom. This is what Paul tells us in Romans. *"For I am not ashamed of the gospel, for it is the power of God for salvation to everyone who believes, to the Jew first and also to the Greek"* (Romans 1:16). The power is in the gospel of Jesus and it needs to be preached to all people.

We need to understand that demons tremble at the name of Jesus (cf. James 2:19) because they know not only who He is, but the power He wields! We need to comprehend that the gospel is very powerful and as such has the ability to change people from the dead and dying to those alive and living in the Name of Jesus.

There is no greater power in the entire universe than God's power. *"For the word of God is living and active and sharper than any two-edged sword, and piercing as far as the division of soul and spirit, of both joints and marrow, and able to judge the thoughts and intentions of the heart. And there is no creature hidden from His sight, but all things are open and laid bare to the eyes of Him with whom we have to do"* (Hebrew 4:12-13). No demon can stand against it. No other human being can withstand Him. Souls need to be saved. Are you for Christ or against Him?

Chapter 15
For the Non-Christian

"For all have sinned, and come short of the glory of God." – Romans 3:23

D o you know *when* you will die? Are you aware of the *day* and *hour* when you will slip from this life into eternity? I'm betting you are not privy to that information. So why are you living as if you **do** *know when it will happen?* Putting a decision about Jesus off until another day is taking a huge chance because of the fact that you do not know when you will die. That is plainly simple, and logic alone demands that you do not put this decision off. Yet you do, because the thought of becoming a Christian makes you feel uncomfortable.

You wrongly believe that to become a Christian means that you have to change in a major way *before* Jesus will accept you. It means to you giving up the things you love now because if you love them, then obviously they are wrong and God does not love them.

You are putting the cart before the horse. You must understand that God is not rejecting you. He is not standing there, tapping His foot, demanding that you eliminate those things that He does not like before you can come to Him for salvation.

If you (or anyone) could do that, you would not *need* His salvation at all. It is because you and I do things that are not pleasing to Him that we need His salvation.

What do you do that you would like to no longer do? Do you drink excessively until you cannot control it? Do you play around with drugs? Do you eat too much food until you have become overweight, lethargic and sickly?

What other things are in your life that you do not like? Are you drawn to illicit extra-marital affairs? Do you have a problem with lust? Are you a shopaholic? Do you tend to tell lies a great deal because it makes you feel important, or to hide things about your life?

Do you find that you do not like people and you would prefer to be around animals or out in the woods than around people? Are you a workaholic? Do you place a high value on money and you find that you work very hard to obtain it?

Here's the problem. The enemy of our souls comes to us and tells us that God will never accept us until we get rid of those things. He lies to us that God essentially wants us "perfect" before He will be willing to meet us and grant us eternal life. This is completely untrue.

The other lie that our enemy tells us is that we should not become a Christian because the fun in our life will fly out the door. We will no longer be able to drink or do the fun things we enjoy now. We start to think that coming to God means becoming a doormat for people and having to fill our life with things we do not want to *ever* do.

These are all lies, and unfortunately, too many people believe them. First of all, God does not expect you to be "perfect" before you come to Him for salvation. If that were the case, no one would be able to ever approach Him.

Secondly, God does not say that He is going to take away all the things we enjoy and replace them with things we hate. What is wrong with enjoying the lake on your boat? What is wrong with spending a day with the family fishing or just relaxing in the mountains? There is nothing wrong with these things.

What God *will* do is begin to remove the things that have ensnared you so that life is actually draining from you, but you are not aware of it. For instance, maybe you drink excessively and you have tried everything you can think of to quit. You have gone to AA meetings, spent thousands of dollars on this program or that, and you have even used your own will power to free yourself from the addiction to alcohol, all to no avail.

The question is not: *do I need to quit before I come to Jesus*? The question is: *am I willing to allow Him to work in and through me to take away the addiction I have to alcohol*? Do you see the difference? Are you willing to allow Him to work in you to break that addiction so that you will become a healthier person, one who is able to think straight and one who learns to rely on Him for strength? That is all He wants you to be able to do. He knows you cannot break that addiction (or any addiction for that matter) with your own strength and willpower. Are you willing to allow Him to do it in and through you?

What if you are a workaholic? What if you have "things" like a boat, a house in Cancun, a large bank account, four cars, and more? Do you think that God is going to ask you to give it up, or worse, do you think that God will simply come in and take all of that from you? I know of nothing in Scripture that tells us He will do that.

What God will do with all of those who come to Him trusting Him for salvation is one thing, which begins the moment we receive salvation and will continue until the day we stand before Him. He will begin to create within us the character of Jesus (cf. Ephesians 2:10).

Here is a verse from the Old Testament that was said originally through the prophet Ezekiel to the people of Israel. While this was specifically stated to the Jews, it is applicable to all who receive salvation through Jesus Christ.

"I will give you a new heart and put a new spirit within you; I will take the heart of stone out of your flesh and give you a heart of flesh. I will put My Spirit within you and cause you to walk in My statutes, and you will keep My judgments and do them" (Ezekiel 36:26-27).

God is speaking here through Ezekiel, and He is saying that He will give the people a new heart of flesh, removing that old heart of stone. This is God's responsibility. God is the One who makes that happen. We are told in the book of Hebrews that God is the Author and Finisher of our faith (cf. Hebrews 12:2). This tells me that God is the One who changes me from within so that over time, my desires are slowly turned into His desires.

I recall years ago thinking that God wanted to do everything in my life that I did not want Him to do. I fell into the asinine belief that He wanted to change everything about me. What I learned is that yes, there are things that God does want to change about me. However, there is a lot that God originally gave me that He has also enhanced and used for His glory.

Maybe you are a workaholic who thinks that working hard is something God does not want you to do. This is not necessarily the case. He may have given you the ability and the knowledge to work in the area of finance for a great purpose. All He may wind up doing is dialing back your workaholic tendencies so that you have more time to enjoy your family and study His Word.

But you say you smoke, or drink, or use illegal drugs, and you don't want to give those up. As I stated, you can't give those up under your own power, and the fact that you have tried so many times has proven it to you.

But God knows what is and what is not good for you. Are you willing to *allow* Him to work in you to change your desires so that you no longer want to smoke, use illegal drugs, or drink nearly as much?

Then you say that you believe God wants to make you a Christian so you can become miserable. Isn't that what most Christians are – miserable? Not the Christians I know, and certainly not me, my wife, or our children.

Where does the Bible say that God wants us miserable? You will not find it. What God wants is for us to be blessed, and that begins when we receive salvation from His hand.

You know, if we would stop and take the time to consider the fact that this life is exceedingly short if we compare it to eternity, we will then realize that there is nothing so important that it should keep us from receiving Jesus as Savior and Lord.

Unfortunately, too many people do not consider the brevity of life. They think they will live forever, or at the very least, they will die when they are really old and gray. That will come too soon. Even though I have just recently turned 54, it still truly seems like yesterday that I was a young boy fishing in the Delaware River near Hobart, New York. There I spent many Saturdays fishing and simply enjoying being outdoors. How did life go by so very quickly? How could that have happened?

It has happened, and I am at a point in life where not only do I realize that this life is short, but I actually look forward to spending eternity with Jesus after this life. Does that sound morbid to you? It shouldn't, because by comparing this life to eternity, we should get a sense of what is truly important.

God does not expect us to become Mother Theresas. He does not necessarily expect us to give up everything and become missionaries in outer Mongolia. What God expects is for us to simply allow Him to change our character as He sees fit.

Over time, we may well find that we have simply stopped swearing without realizing it. Our desire for cigarettes or alcohol has nearly evaporated. Illicit affairs no longer enter the picture.

We also may find that some of the things we want to eliminate in our life become more pronounced. Often the enemy will do this to cause us to focus on something that God is not even doing in our lives at that point. It causes tension, frustration, and self-anger.

If you have gotten to this point in your life and you have not dealt with the question about Jesus, it is about time you do so. You need to stop what you are doing and realize a couple of things before you go through another minute in this life.

- **Sinner**: you need to realize that you are a sinner. You have sinned and you will continue to sin. Sin is breaking the laws that God has set up. We all sin. We have all broken God's laws and that breaks any connection we might have had with God. Sin pushes us away from Him.

Romans 3:23 says, *"For all have sinned, and come short of the glory of God."* That means you and that means me. All means all. That is the first step. We need to recognize and agree with God that yes, we are sinners. I'm a sinner. You are a sinner. This results in God's anger, what the Bible terms "wrath."

- **God's Wrath**: Romans 1:18 says, *"For the wrath of God is revealed from heaven against all ungodliness and unrighteousness of men, who suppress the truth in unrighteousness."*

This is as much a fact as the truth that we are all sinners. Because we are sinners – by breaking God's law(s) – God has every right to be angry with us and ultimately destroy that which is sinful. If we choose to remain "in" our sinful states throughout this life, we will – unfortunately – be destroyed with the rest of sin.

Fortunately, there *is* a remedy, and it is salvation.

- **God's Gift**: In the sixteenth chapter of Acts, a jailer asks Paul this famous question: *what must I do to be saved?* The question was asked because Paul and Barnabas had been imprisoned, and while there, they began singing praises to God.

God then sent a powerful earthquake that opened the doors to all the prison cells, yet no one escaped. When the jailer arrived, he saw that everyone was still in their cells, and after seeing that miracle (what prisoner would not want to escape from prison?), turned and asked what he must do to be saved. He was speaking of the spiritual aspect of things. He wanted to know how he could be guaranteed eternal life.

The answer Paul gave the man was, "*Believe on the Lord Jesus Christ, and thou shalt be saved, and thy house*" (Acts 16:31).

This is not head knowledge or intellectual assent. This is *believing from the heart*. In fact, Paul makes a very similar statement in another book he wrote, Romans. He says, "*That if thou shalt confess with thy mouth the Lord Jesus, and shalt believe in thine heart that God hath raised him from the dead, thou shalt be saved. For with the heart man believeth unto righteousness; and with the mouth confession is made unto salvation*" (Romans 10:9-10).

When we fully believe something, we confess that it is true. It must begin in the heart because that is where the will is located. We must want to believe. We must endeavor to believe. We must seek to believe.

We must stop giving ourselves all the reasons to deny or ignore Jesus. As God, He became a Man, born of a virgin. He clothed Himself with humanity that He might show us how to live, and in so doing, would keep every portion of the law.

If Jesus was capable of keeping every portion of the law, then He would be found worthy to become a sacrifice for our sin – yours and mine. If He became a sacrifice for our sin, then all that we must do is embrace Him and His sacrificial death.

In short then, to become saved we must:

1. Admit (we sin)
2. Repent (want to turn away from it)
3. Believe (that Jesus is the answer)
4. Embrace (the truth about Jesus)

We **admit** that we are sinner, that we have sinned. This is nothing more than agreeing with God that we have broken His law. Can you honestly say that you have not broken God's law? If you admit to breaking even the "smallest" law, then you are a lawbreaker.

After we admit that we have sinned, the next step is found in **repenting**. Some believe that repenting is actually moving away from sin. This author believes that it is a willingness to move away from sin, and there is a difference.

As we have already discussed, it is impossible to stop sinning. Human beings simply cannot do it because as long as we live, we will have a sin nature, which is something within us that gives us a propensity to sin. As long as we have this inner propensity to sin or break God's laws, we will never be perfect in this life.

We cannot one day say, "Lord, I promise to stop sinning." If we do that, we are only kidding ourselves and setting ourselves up for major failure. We cannot stop sinning in this life. The most we can do is *want* to stop sinning and then spend the rest of our lives allowing God to create the character of Jesus within us, slowly, little by little.

Repenting is to decide that you no longer want to do the things that keep us out of heaven. We no longer wish to break God's laws. It is not promising God that we will never sin again.

Once we admit, then repent, we must **believe**. This is one of the most difficult things to do because believing that Jesus died in our place, that He lived a perfectly sinless life, is extremely difficult to believe. Our minds cannot grasp that truth. We must ask God to open our eyes to that truth so that we can embrace it.

While on the cross next to Jesus, the one thief joined the other thief in ridiculing Jesus. Then, all of a sudden – as we read in Luke 23 – this same thief that had just been ridiculing Him now turned to Him with a new understanding.

It was this new understanding that prompted the thief to say to Jesus, *"Lord, remember me when you come into your Kingdom."* Jesus looked at the man and responded to him, *"Today, you will be with me in paradise."*

What had occurred in the mind and heart of that thief from one moment to the next? One thing, and that one thing was that God opened the thief's eyes so that he could see the truth. It was as if the blinders fell off and he now saw and understood who Jesus was, even to the most cursory degree that Jesus was dying not for Himself, but for others.

It was this understanding, this awareness, which prompted the man to ask Jesus to simply be remembered. Jesus went way beyond it to promise the man that he would be with Jesus that day in paradise.

Please notice in Luke 23 that there is nothing in the chapter that tells us that the man promised Jesus he would give up sin, or that he would never sin again. There is nothing that tells us that thief took the time to enter into a final deathbed confession of his sins so that he could be absolved.

The thief made no promises to Jesus at all. What he experienced was the truth of who Jesus was and what Jesus accomplished for humanity. Jesus accomplished what we cannot. What is left is for each person to *admit, repent, believe,* and *embrace*.

Let me clarify here that though we do not see any verbal repentance from the thief, we know that he did repent. He admitted as well. How can we know this? Simply due to the thief's complete about-face with respect to his attitude toward Jesus. One minute, he was ridiculing Jesus, and the next, embracing Him. This is important. There is no way he could have or would have *embraced* Jesus had he not been humbled by the truth *about* Jesus.

Once the thief saw the truth, he was instantly humbled. Within himself, he knew that he was a sinner, and in fact the text states that this is what he told the other thief dying next to him. *"But the other answering rebuked him, saying, Dost not thou fear God, seeing thou art in the same condemnation? And we indeed justly; for we receive the due reward of our deeds: but this man hath done nothing amiss"* (Luke 23:40-41). Something happened within the heart of the one thief. In one moment, the thief went from harassing Jesus to recognizing his own sinfulness, and then ultimately asking for grace, which was freely given to him.

Whether he said it or not, the thief went from haughtiness to humility in a very short space of time, and it was all because he saw the truth about Jesus. That truth helped him realize that he deserved his death and what would happen to him after death. He understood that Jesus did not deserve death.

From here, the thief fully embraced the truth about Jesus and was rewarded with eternal life because of it. He did not come off the cross to be water baptized. He did not list a long litany of offenses against God. He recognized the truth about Jesus, was humbled, and embraced that truth!

This is what each of us needs to do. We cannot give in to the lie that tells us that we are not good enough, or we have not given up enough before God will accept us. We must reject the lie that says we must somehow earn our salvation.

Jesus has done everything that is necessary to make salvation available to us. The only thing that is left for us is to see the truth. Once we see that truth, it should humble us to the point of embracing Jesus and all that He stands for and is to us.

The eighth chapter of Romans begins with the fact that all who trust Jesus for salvation are no longer condemned...*ever*. All of my sins –

past, present, and future – have not only been forgiven, but canceled. It is because of my faith in the atonement (death) of Jesus that God is able to cancel all of my sins, even the ones that I have not committed yet. This does not make me eager to commit them. It makes me want to do what I can to avoid sinning.

If you do not know Jesus, please do not put down this book without deliberately *believing* that He is God, that He died for you by the shedding of His blood on the cross, and that He rose three days later because death could not keep Him. Do you believe that? If you do not yet believe it, do you *want* to believe it? If so, then simply ask God to help you come to believe all that Jesus is and all that He has accomplished for you. God will answer your prayers and you may either receive instantaneous awareness of all that Jesus is and has done, or it may be a *growing* awareness over time. In either case, it is the most important decision you will ever make.

Turn to Him now and pray for knowledge of the truth and an ability to embrace it. Please. He is waiting for you.

Ask Yourself:

1. Do you *know* Jesus? Are you in *relationship* with Him? Have you had a spiritual transaction according to John 3?
2. Do you *want* to receive eternal life through the only salvation that is available?
3. Do you believe that Jesus is God the Son, who was born of a virgin, lived a sinless life, died a bloody and gruesome death to pay for your sin, was buried, and rose again on the third day? Do you *believe* this?
4. Do you *want* to *embrace* the truth from #3?
5. Pray that God will open your eyes and provide you with the faith to begin believing the truth about Jesus. Ask Him to help your faith embrace the truth, realizing that you are not good

enough to save yourself and that your sin will keep you out of God's Kingdom without His salvation.
6. Pray as if your life depended upon it because *it does*!

Visit our page on **SermonAudio.com/study-grow-know** to hear our latest broadcasts as well as those that have been archived.

Those who understand the Bible in literal terms are constantly accused of not understanding the Bible in literal terms.

Someone will point to the word "all" or "this" or "that" and charge that the Literalist does not take those words literally, therefore they are not truly understanding the Bible in literal terms.

Is there any truth to this? Does the Literalist strive to understand the literal meaning of the Bible, and by doing so, is he required to understand every word in its most literal sense? ($12.99; 142 pages, ISBN: 978-1441487568)

Christians should always be ready to present the reason for the hope that we have in Christ. However, this is completely different than attempting to win people with arguments and words. What we often fail to remember is that the Holy Spirit is deeply involved in the process of saving souls. We need to rely less on ourselves and more on Him. Either He opens eyes, or He does not.

($11.99; 124 pages, ISBN: 978-0977424467)

Being a Christian is not necessarily a walk in the park. While it begins with the new birth Jesus spoke about with Nicodemus (John 3), this is just the starting point of a lifetime of setting Self's will to the side in favor of fulfilling Christ's will.

($10.99; 100 pages, ISBN: 978-1442110908)

You have to wonder sometimes. Though the visible church is being overrun by Contemplative Prayer, Church Growth movements, Seeker-Sensitive thinking, the Emergent Church, Spiritual Formation and a host of dangerous philosophies that are squelching the authentic gospel with what Paul would call "another" gospel, there are far too many individuals who seem unable to see the forest for the trees.   ($13.99; 204 pages, ISBN: 978-0982644317)

Many think they know Dispensationalism and many believe it to be heretical, with some even viewing it as a cult. What is the truth about normative Dispensationalism? This book addresses some of the charges against it in question and short answer format.

($13.99; 194 pages, ISBN: 978-1448632404)

Because of the nature of the times we live in, it is natural to discuss areas of Eschatology (study of End Times). So many events and situations seem to point to the fact that the Tribulation period is right around the corner. During these discussions, all aspects of the End Times are routinely examined, including the timing of the Rapture, the arrival of the Antichrist, the Millennial Reign of Jesus, the coming Gog-Magog (Attempted) Invasion of Israel, and the list goes on.   ($13.99; 152 pages, ISBN: 978-0982644386)

A phenomenon is happening today at an alarming rate. More and more people are boldly proclaiming that they are no longer Christians but "ex-Christians." Many are now, in fact, atheists.

Can this be true? If they are non-Christians now, were they truly Christians to begin with? They will state without equivocation that they were in fact committed Christians, but no longer are. What is the deal?

($14.99; 240 pages, ISBN: 978-1442100817)

It should be apparent to every believer that God has one supreme, overarching purpose for everything He does. Every plan He puts in motion, whether directly or by allowing it to occur, is done with that ultimate, singular purpose in mind. The natural question then becomes, what is God's singular highest purpose for everything He has accomplished, is accomplishing, or will accomplish? Is it found in the plan of redemption?   ($14.99; 224 pages, ISBN: 978-1442163676)

Anything that is seen as opposing Islam is considered an enemy. Under Islam and its Shariah law, no mercy is extended to those who stand in the way of Islam's encroachment. Those who do not convert to Islam will be executed.

The most recent phenomenon is seen in the blending of Christianity with Islam, something many have been calling Chrislam. This idea that Muslims can worship with Christians and vice versa is completely rejected by Scripture, which states that there is only one way to receive authentic salvation. It is through Jesus: Savior, Lord, and God.

($13.99; 126 pages, ISBN: 978-0983700678

Don't have the money to buy books? Our books are available **FREE** of charge as downloadable PDF documents from our webpage.

Just click on each book's cover and look for the PDF icon for that book. Click it and download! It's free.

Behind Enemy Lines

Four verses in the ninth chapter of Daniel are arguably some of the most important verses related to prophecy found anywhere in Scripture. If we are to understand what God has given us in these four verses, then we had better do all that we can to ensure we have a correct interpretation.

The 70 weeks of Daniel, highlighted in Daniel 9:24-27, are there for our benefit. God did not need to tell us anything, but He chose to do so in order that we would be blessed by the information He has graciously provided to Daniel through the angel Gabriel.

($10.99; 77 pages, ISBN: 978-1442189546)

Rather than simply attempting to deal with aspects of this subject which have already been dealt with, author Fred DeRuvo tackles the claims against the PreTrib Rapture from another perspective.

He deals with the plausibility of a few men being able to pull off what has got to be the greatest hoax the church has ever known...if it actually was a hoax. Beyond this, DeRuvo also deals with many other claims by the Anti-PreTrib Rapturist, finding out if these claims hold any water at all. ($13.99; 168 pages, ISBN: 978-0982644300)

There is huge disagreement about just exactly how Christians are to view their own sin. Some say there needs to be a continual awareness of how bad we are because of our sin and that we need to express absolute remorse to God whenever we commit a sin. If we do not, then God will not take us seriously and sin will not be forgiven.

($11.99; 136 pages, ISBN: 978-0983700647)

What is it that causes people to want to know the secret things of the universe, whether they are true or not? Clearly, knowledge is power, and power can feel absolute when it is kept within a cloistered group.

It appears as though there has been a deliberately hidden, yet clear, goal, known only to those who have been initiated within the various esoteric societies that have existed throughout the ages. These societies use secrecy to draw in those who seek power and dominion over the entire earth through coming cataclysmic changes. ($13.99; 182 pages, ISBN: 978-0983700661)

Behind Enemy Lines

There is a chaos coming that is predicated upon the rise of Islam, Satanic Soldiers, aliens, and evil beyond measure. As an ideology, Islam masquerades as a religious light to the world, one that promises to usher in world peace – but at what cost? Through the use of political strategies, military might, and religious tenets, adherents of Islam work within various established governments to create special laws or exemptions for Muslims in the hope of eventually overthrowing that established government. Can it happen? IS it happening? Find out in *Evil Rising*. ($13.95; 184 pages, ISBN: 978-0977424429)

We hear all the time how bad things are getting throughout the world. Do we chalk it all up to being the normal cycles that occur in life, or is something else going on behind the scenes? What if this generation alive now turns out to be the last one before Jesus returns? Is there any truth at all to the claim that Jesus will return one day? If you are one who has not taken the time to read through some of the books of the Bible that are said to teach truths regarding the last days, *Living in the Last Generation* puts it out there in a straightforward manner, making it easy to understand. ($11.95; 132 pages, ISBN: 978-0977424405)

ALIENology is somewhat of a science for many who believe that entities from other planets or dimensions enter and leave our dimensions at will. What can we learn from these beings? Anything truthful? Dr. Fred believes that putting our faith in anything these beings say may be a huge leap in the wrong direction. Aliens reportedly come in all shapes, sizes, and even cultural representations. Because of this, there tends to be a good deal of mixed messages out there, yet people believe it because of their experience. Anything wrong with that picture? ($14.99; 176 pages, ISBN: 978-0983700609)

Raised for His Glory delves into the books of Ezekiel and Romans to determine what the Bible actually says about Israel. Is the section on Ezekiel 36-39 speaking of a future time when nations will gather against Israel, or is this something that has already occurred? Moreover, just exactly what is the Valley of the Dry Bones referring to – the nation of Israel, or the Church? Join Dr. Fred as he presents his understanding of these very important sections of God's Word and how they relate to the only nation that He ever created, Israel. ($15.99; 190 pages, ISBN: 978-0983700623)

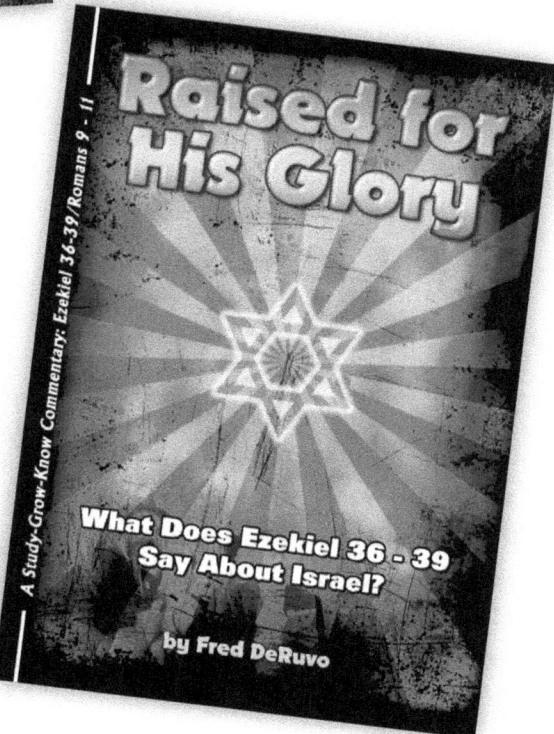

Society has changed drastically over the past decades. Why is that? Simply due to the fact that people have become more preoccupied with *Self*. In this book, Dr. Fred presents *Self* as an entity capable of getting things done its way and using the individual to accomplish it.

In essence, Self easily becomes the master to every person who is not under the control of God's Holy Spirit, with the person becoming the slave. ($14.99; 206 pages, ISBN: 978-0983700630)

In this commentary on Revelation, author Fred DeRuvo draws back the curtain on chapters five through twenty-two, presenting information in an easy-to-understand style, written for the average person. One thing is certain regarding the book of Revelation. Because of its prophetic nature, Christians will continue to debate aspects of it until such a time as we can know for certain. Either the things found within Revelation are yet to come to pass, and that alone will prove their veracity, or they will not come to *pass. Only time will tell.* ($18.00; 392 pages, ISBN: 978-0977424498)

The book of Jude is only twenty-five verses in length, but it packs a spiritual wallop! Jude, the brother of James (and half-brother of our Lord Jesus), writes a message to believers about the times in which they lived. Those times are not at all that much different from the days in which we now live. Jude warns against apostasy, licentiousness, and the mockers that are destined to be part of the last days. Even during Jude's day, mocking the Lord's return had already begun. How much worse is it today, roughly 2,000 years later? ($11.99; 126 pages, ISBN: 978-0983700692)

Everyone has an opinion. It does not matter whether you're a New Ager, a UFO researcher, a student of the Bible, or simply a curious party. Theories regarding aliens range from believing that the whole alien phenomenon is nothing more than an elaborate hoax, to the belief that they are real and getting ready to take over our world, to the view that they are demons disguising themselves as aliens.

($15.99; 206 pages, ISBN: 978-0982644393)

Moo!

www.ingramcontent.com/pod-product-compliance
Lightning Source LLC
Chambersburg PA
CBHW080436110426
42743CB00016B/3187